Tucholsky Wagner Zola Fonatne Sydow Freud Schlegel
Turgenev Wallace
Twain Walther von der Vogelweide Fouqué Friedrich II. von Preußen
Weber Freiligrath Frey
Fechner Fichte Weiße Rose von Fallersleben Kant Ernst Frommel
Richthofen
Hölderlin
Engels Fielding Eichendorff Tacitus Dumas
Fehrs Faber Flaubert
Eliasberg Ebner Eschenbach
Feuerbach Maximilian I. von Habsburg Fock Eliot Zweig
Ewald Vergil
Goethe Elisabeth von Österreich London
Mendelssohn Balzac Shakespeare Dostojewski Ganghofer
Trackl Lichtenberg Rathenau Doyle Gjellerup
Stevenson Hambruch
Mommsen Tolstoi Lenz Droste-Hülshoff
Thoma Hanrieder
Dach Verne von Arnim Hägele Hauff Humboldt
Reuter Rousseau Hagen Hauptmann Gautier
Karrillon Garschin Baudelaire
Damaschke Defoe Hebbel
Descartes Hegel Kussmaul Herder
Wolfram von Eschenbach Dickens Schopenhauer Rilke George
Bronner Darwin Melville Grimm Jerome Bebel
Campe Horváth Aristoteles Proust
Bismarck Vigny Barlach Voltaire Federer Herodot
Gengenbach Heine
Storm Casanova Tersteegen Grillparzer Georgy
Chamberlain Lessing Langbein Gilm Gryphius
Brentano Lafontaine
Strachwitz Claudius Schiller Kralik Iffland Sokrates
Katharina II. von Rußland Bellamy Schilling
Gerstäcker Raabe Gibbon Tschechow
Löns Hesse Hoffmann Gogol Wilde Gleim Vulpius
Luther Heym Hofmannsthal Klee Hölty Morgenstern
Roth Heyse Klopstock Goedicke
Luxemburg Puschkin Homer Kleist
Machiavelli La Roche Horaz Mörike Musil
Navarra Aurel Musset Kierkegaard Kraft Kraus
Lamprecht Kind Hugo Moltke
Nestroy Marie de France Kirchhoff
Laotse Ipsen Liebknecht
Nietzsche Nansen Ringelnatz
Marx Lassalle Gorki Klett Leibniz
von Ossietzky May vom Stein Lawrence Irving
Petalozzi Knigge
Platon Pückler Michelangelo Kafka
Sachs Poe Liebermann Kock
Korolenko
de Sade Praetorius Mistral Zetkin

The publishing house tredition has created the series **TREDITION CLASSICS**. It contains classical literature works from over two thousand years. Most of these titles have been out of print and off the bookstore shelves for decades.

The book series is intended to preserve the cultural legacy and to promote the timeless works of classical literature. As a reader of a **TREDITION CLASSICS** book, the reader supports the mission to save many of the amazing works of world literature from oblivion.

The symbol of **TREDITION CLASSICS** is Johannes Gutenberg (1400 – 1468), the inventor of movable type printing.

With the series, tredition intends to make thousands of international literature classics available in printed format again – worldwide.

All books are available at book retailers worldwide in paperback and in hardcover. For more information please visit: www.tredition.com

tredition was established in 2006 by Sandra Latusseck and Soenke Schulz. Based in Hamburg, Germany, tredition offers publishing solutions to authors and publishing houses, combined with worldwide distribution of printed and digital book content. tredition is uniquely positioned to enable authors and publishing houses to create books on their own terms and without conventional manufacturing risks.

For more information please visit: www.tredition.com

Life in a Tank

Richard Haigh

Imprint

This book is part of the TREDITION CLASSICS series.

Author: Richard Haigh
Cover design: toepferschumann, Berlin (Germany)

Publisher: tredition GmbH, Hamburg (Germany)
ISBN: 978-3-8491-4888-1

www.tredition.com
www.tredition.de

Contents

Illustrations

A Tank on its Way into Action
British Official Photograph
King George and Queen Mary inspecting a Tank on
the British Front in France
British Official Photograph
A British Tank and its Crew in New York
Photograph by Underwood & Underwood
A Tank moving to the Attack down what was once a
Main Street
British Official Photograph
A Tank going over a Trench on its Way into Action
British Official Photograph
A Tank halfway over the Top and awaiting the Order
to Advance in the Battle of Menin Road
Photograph by Underwood & Underwood
A Tank bringing in a Captured German Gun under
Protection of Camouflage
Photograph by Underwood & Underwood
A British Tank in the Liberty Loan Parade in New
York
Photograph by Underwood & Underwood

[1]

LIFE IN A TANK

I

THE MEANING OF THE TANK CORPS

TANKS!

To the uninitiated—as were we in those days when we returned to the Somme, too late to see the tanks make their first dramatic entrance—the name conjures up a picture of an iron monster, breathing fire and exhaling bullets and shells, hurling itself against the enemy, unassailable by man and impervious to the most deadly engines of war; sublime, indeed, in its expression of indomitable power and resolution.

This picture was one of the two factors which attracted us toward the Heavy Branch Machine-Gun Corps—as the Tank Corps was known in the first year of its being. On the Somme we had seen a derelict tank, wrecked, despoiled of her guns, and forsaken in No [2] Man's Land. We had swarmed around and over her, wild with curiosity, much as the Lilliputians must have swarmed around the prostrate Gulliver. Our imagination was fired.

The second factor was, frankly, that we were tired of going over the top as infantrymen. The first time that a man goes into an attack, he as a rule enjoys it. He has no conception of its horrors,—no, not horrors, for war possesses no horrors,—but, rather, he has no knowledge of the sudden realization of the sweetness of life that comes to a man when he is "up against it." The first time, it is a splendid, ennobling novelty. And as for the "show" itself, in actual practice it is more like a dream which only clarifies several days later, after it is all over. But to do the same thing a second and third and fourth time, is to bring a man face to face with Death in its fullest and most realistic uncertainty. In soldier jargon he "gets most awful wind up." It is five minutes before "Zero Hour." All preparations are complete. You are waiting for the signal to hop over the parapet. Very probably the Boche knows that you are [3] coming, and is already skimming the sandbags with his machine guns and knocking little pieces of earth and stone into your face. Extraordinary, how maddening is the sting of these harmless little pebbles and bits of dirt! The bullets ricochet away with a peculiar singing hiss, or crack overhead when they go too high. The shells which burst on the other side of the parapet shake the ground with a dull thud and crash. There are two minutes to wait before going over. Then is the time when a man feels a sinking sensation in his stomach; when his hands tremble ever so slightly, and when he offers up a pathetic little prayer to God that if he's a bit of a sportsman he may be spared from death, should his getting through not violate the divine and fatalistic plans. He has that unpleasant lack of knowledge of what comes beyond. For after all, with the most intense belief in the world, it is hard to reconcile the comforting feeling of what one knows with that terrible dread of the unknown.

A man has no great and glorious ideas that nothing matters because he is ready to die for [4] his country. He is, of course, ready to die for her. But he does not think about it. He lights a cigarette and tries to be nonchalant, for he knows that his men are watching him, and it is his duty to keep up a front for their sake. Probably, at the same time, they are keeping up a front for him. Then the Sergeant Major comes along, cool and smiling, as if he were out for a stroll at home. Suddenly he is an immense comfort. One forgets that sinking feeling in the stomach and thinks, "How easy and jolly he is! What a splendid fellow!" Immediately, one begins unconsciously to imitate him. Then another thinks the same thing about one, and begins to imitate too. So it passes on, down the line. But there is nothing heroic or exalting in going over the top.

This, then, was our possible second reason for preferring to attack inside bullet-proof steel; not that death is less likely in a tank, but there seems to be a more sporting chance with a shell than with a bullet. The enemy infantryman looks along his sight and he has you for a certainty, but the gunner cannot be so accurate [5] and twenty yards may mean a world of difference. Above all, the new monster had our imaginations in thrall. Here were novelty and wonderful developments.

In the end of 1916, therefore, a certain number of officers and men received their orders to join the H.B.M.G.C., and proceeded sorrowfully and joyfully away from the trenches. Sorrowfully, because it is a poor thing to leave your men and your friends in danger, and get out of it yourself into something new and fresh; joyfully, because one is, after all, but human.

About thirty miles behind the line some villages were set aside for the housing and training of the new units. Each unit had a nucleus of men who had already served in tanks, with the new arrivals spread around to make up to strength.

The new arrivals came from all branches of the Service; Infantry, Sappers, Gunners, Cavalry, and the Army Service Corps. Each man was very proud of his own Branch; and a wonderfully healthy rivalry and affection [6] sprang up between them. The gunner twitted the sapper, the cavalryman made jokes at the A.S.C., and the infantryman groused at the whole lot. But all knew at the bottom of their hearts, how each is essential to the other.

It was to be expected when all these varied men came together, that the inculcating of a proper *esprit de corps* — the training of each individual in an entirely new science for the benefit of the whole — would prove a very difficult and painstaking task. But the wonderful development, however, in a few months, of a large, heterogeneous collection of men into a solid, keen, self-sacrificing unit, was but another instance of the way in which war improves the character and temperament of man.

It was entirely new for men who were formerly in a regiment, full of traditions, to find themselves in the Tank Corps. Here was a Corps, the functions of which resulted from an idea born of the exigencies of this science-demanding war. Unlike every other branch of the Service, it has no regimental history to direct it, no traditions upon which to build, and still [7] more important from a practical point of view, no experience from which to draw for guidance, either in training or in action. In the Infantry, the attack has resulted from a steady development in ideas and tactics, with past wars to give a foundation and this present one to suggest changes and to bring about remedies for the defects which crop up daily. With this new weapon, which was launched on the Somme on September 15, 1916, the tactics had to be decided upon with no realistic experimentation as ground work; and, moreover, with the very difficult task of working in concert with other arms of the Service that had had two years of fighting, from which to learn wisdom.

With regard to discipline, too, — of all things the most important, for the success of a battle has depended, does, and always will depend, upon the state of discipline of the troops engaged, — all old regiments have their staff of regular instructors to drill and teach recruits. In them has grown up that certain feeling and loyalty which time and past deeds have done so much to foster and cherish. Here were [8] we, lacking traditions, history, and experience of any kind.

It is easy to realize the responsibility that lay not only upon the Chief of this new Corps, but upon each individual and lowest member thereof. It was for us all to produce *esprit de corps*, and to produce it quickly. It was necessary for us to develop a love of the work, not because we felt it was worth while, but because we knew that success or failure depended on each man's individual efforts.

But, naturally, the real impetus came from the top, and no admiration or praise can be worthy of that small number of men in whose hands the real destinies of this new formation lay; who were continually devising new schemes and ideas for binding the whole together, and for turning that whole into a highly efficient, up-to-date machine.

KING GEORGE AND QUEEN MARY INSPECTING A TANK ON THE BRITISH FRONT IN FRANCE ToList

"How did the tank happen to be invented?" is a common question. The answer is that in past wars experience has made it an axiom that the defenders suffer more casualties than the attacking forces From the first days of 1914, [9] however, this condition was reversed, and whole waves of attacking troops were mown down by two or three machine guns, each manned, possibly, by not more than three men. There may be in a certain sector, before an attack, an enormous preliminary bombardment which is destined to knock out guns, observation posts, dumps, men, and above all, machine-gun emplacements. Nevertheless, it has been found in actual practice that despite the most careful observation and equally careful study of aeroplane photographs, there are, as a rule, just one or two machine guns which, either through bad luck or through precautions on the part of the enemy, have escaped destruction. These are the guns which inflict the damage when the infantrymen go over and which may hold up a whole attack.

It was thought, therefore, that a machine might be devised which would cross shell-craters, wire and trenches, and be at the same time impervious to bullets, and which would contain a certain

number of guns to be used for knocking out such machine guns as
were [10] still in use, or to lay low the enemy infantry. With this
idea, a group of men, in the end of 1915, devised the present type of
heavy armoured car. In order to keep the whole plan as secret as
possible, about twenty-five square miles of ground in Great Britain
were set aside and surrounded with armed guards. There, through
all the spring and early summer of 1916, the work was carried on,
without the slightest hint of its existence reaching the outside world.
Then, one night, the tanks were loaded up and shipped over to
France, to make that first sensational appearance on the Somme,
with the success which warranted their further production on a
larger and more ambitious scale.

[11]

II

FIRST DAYS OF TRAINING ToC

We were at a rest camp on the Somme when the chit first came round regarding the joining of the H.B.M.G.C. The Colonel came up to us one day with some papers in his hand.

"Does anybody want to join this?" he asked.

We all crowded around to find out what "this" might be.

"Tanks!" some one cried. Some were facetious; others indifferent; a few mildly interested. But no one seemed very keen about it, especially as the tanks in those days had a reputation for rather heavy casualties. Only Talbot, remembering the derelict and the interest she had inspired, said, with a laugh,—

"I rather think I'll put my name down, sir. Nothing will come of it, but one might just as well try." And taking one of the papers he filled it in, while the others stood around making all the remarks appropriate to such an occasion.

[12] Two or three weeks went by and Talbot had forgotten all about it, in the more absorbing events which crowded months into days on the Somme.

One day the Adjutant came up to him and, smiling, put out his hand.

"Well, good-bye, Talbot. Good luck."

When a man puts out his hand and says "Good-bye," you naturally take the proffered hand and say "Good-bye," too. Talbot found himself saying "Good-bye" before he realized what he was doing. Then he laughed.

"Now that I've said 'Good-bye,' where am I going?" he asked.

"To the Tanks," the Adjutant replied.

So he was really to go; really to leave behind his battalion, his friends, his men, and his servant. For a moment the Somme and the camp seemed the most desirable places on earth. He thought he must have been a fool the day he signed that paper signifying his desire to join another Corps. But it was done now. There were his orders in the Colonel's hand.

[13] "When do I start, sir? And where do I go?" he asked.

"You're to leave immediately for B— —, wherever that is. Take your horse as far as the railhead and get a train for B— —, where the Tank Headquarters are. Good-bye, Talbot; I'm sorry to lose you." A silent handshake, and they parted.

Talbot's kit was packed and sent off on the transport. A few minutes later he was shaking hands all round. His spirits were rising at the thought of this new adventure, but it was a wrench, leaving his regiment. It was, in a way, he thought, as if he were turning his back on an old friend. The face of Dobbin, his groom, as he brought the horses round was not conducive to cheer. He must get the business over and be off. So he mounted and rode off through a gray, murky drizzle, to the railhead about eight miles away. There came the parting with Dobbin and with his pony. Horses mean as much as men sometimes, and his had worked so nobly with him through the mud on the Somme. He wondered if there would [14] be any one in the new place who would be so faithful to him as Polly. Finally, there was Dobbin riding away, back to M— —, with the horse, and its empty saddle, trotting along beside him. It was simply rotten leaving them all!

One has, however, little time for introspection in the Army, and especially when one engages in a tilt with an R.T.O. The R.T.O. has been glorified by an imaginative soul with the title of "Royal Transportation Officer." As a matter of fact, the "R" does not stand for "royal," but for "railway," and the "T" is "transport," nothing so grandiose as "transportation." Now an R.T.O.'s job, though it may be a safe one, is not enviable. He is forced to combine the qualities of booking-clerk, station-master, goods-agent, information clerk, and day and night watchman all into one. In consequence of this it is necessary for the traveller's speech and attitude to be strictly soothing and complimentary. Talbot's obsession at this moment was as to whether B— — was near or far back from the line.

[15] If he supposed that B— — was "near" the line, the R.T.O. might tell him—just to prove how kind Fate is—that it was a good many miles in the rear. But no such luck. The R.T.O. coldly informed Talbot that he hadn't the slightest idea where B— — was. He only knew that trains went there. And, by the way, the trains didn't go there direct. It would be necessary for him to change at Boulogne. Talbot noticed these signs of thawing with delight. And to change at Boulogne! Life was brighter.

Travelling in France in the northern area, at the present time, would seem to be a refutation of the truth that a straight line is the shortest distance between two points. For in order to arrive at one's destination, it is usually necessary to go about sixty miles out of one's way,—hence the necessity for Talbot's going to Boulogne in order to get a train running north.

He arrived at Boulogne only to find that the train for B— — left in an hour.

He strolled out into the streets. Boulogne had then become the Mecca for all those in [16] search of gaiety. Here were civilized people once again. And a restaurant with linen and silver and shining glass, and the best dinner he had ever eaten.

When he had paid his bill and gone out, he stopped at the corner of the street just to look at the people passing by. A large part of the monotony of this war is occasioned, of course, by the fact that the soldier sees nothing but the everlasting drab of uniforms. When a man is in the front line, or just behind, for weeks at a time he sees nothing but soldiers, soldiers, soldiers! Each man has the same coloured uniform; each has the same pattern tunic, the same puttees. Each is covered with the same mud for days at a time. It is the occasion for a thrill when a "Brass Hat" arrives, for he at least has the little brilliant red tabs on his tunic! A man sometimes finds himself envying the soldiers of the old days who could have occasional glimpses of the dashing uniforms of their officers, and although a red coat makes a target of a man, the colour is at least more cheerful than the eternal khaki. The old-time [17] soldier had his red coat and his bands, blaring encouragingly. The soldier of to-day has his drab and no music at all, unless he sings. And every man in an army is not gifted with a voice.

So Talbot looked with joy on the charming dresses and still more charming faces of the women and girls who passed him. Even the men in their civilian clothes were good to look upon.

Riding on French trains is very soothing unless one is in a hurry. But unlike a man in civil life, the soldier has no interest in the speed of trains. The civilian takes it as a personal affront if his train is a few minutes late, or if it does not go as fast as he thinks it should. But the soldier can afford to let the Government look after such minor details. The train moved along at a leisurely pace through the lovely French countryside, making frequent friendly stops at way-side stations. On the platform at Étaples station was posted a rhyme which read:—

> "A wise old owl lived in an oak,
> The more he saw, the less he spoke;
> The less he spoke, the more he heard;
> Soldiers should imitate that old bird."

[18] It was the first time that Talbot had seen this warlike ditty. Its intention was to guard soldiers from saying too much in front of strangers. Talbot vowed, however, to apply its moral to himself at all times and under all conditions.

From nine in the morning until half-past two in the afternoon they rolled along, and had covered by this time the extraordinary distance of about forty miles! Here at last was the station of Saint-P— —.

Talbot looked about him. Standing near was an officer with the Machine-Gun Corps Badge, whom he hailed, and questioned about the Headquarters of the Tank Corps.

"About ten miles from here. Are you going there?" the fellow asked.

Talbot explained that he hoped to, and being saturated with Infantry ideas, he wondered if a passing motor lorry might give him a lift.

The man laughed. "Why don't you telephone Headquarters and ask them to send a car over for you?" he asked.

Talbot did not quite know whether the [19] fellow were ragging him or not. He decided that he was, for who had ever heard of "telephoning for a car"?

"Oh, I don't believe I'll do that—thanks very much for the hint, all the same," he said. "Just tell me which road to take and I'll be quite all right."

The officer smiled.

"I'm quite serious about it," he said. "We all telephone for cars when we need them. There's really no point in your walking—in fact, they'll be surprised if you stroll in upon them. Try telephoning and you'll find they won't die of shock."

Partly to see whether they would or not, and partly because he found the prospect of a motor car more agreeable than a ten-mile walk, Talbot telephoned. Here he experienced another pleasant surprise, for he was put through to Headquarters with no difficulty at all. A cheerful voice answered and he stated his case.

"Cheero," the voice replied. "We'll have a car there for you in an hour—haven't one now, but there will be one ready shortly."

[20] Saint-P— — was a typical French town, and Talbot strolled around. There were soldiers everywhere, but the town had never seen the Germans, and it was a pleasant place. There was, too, a refreshing lack of thick mud—at least it was not a foot deep.

Although Talbot could not quite believe that the car would materialize, it proved to be a substantial fact in the form of a box-body, and in about an hour he was speeding toward Headquarters. It was dark when they reached the village, and as they entered, he experienced that curious feeling of apprehensive expectancy with which one approaches the spot where one is to live and work for some time to come. The car slowed up to pass some carts on the road, and started forward with such a jerk that Talbot was precipitated from the back of the machine into the road. He picked himself up, covered with mud. The solemn face of the driver did not lessen his discomfiture. Here was a strange village, strange men, and he was covered with mud!

A BRITISH TANK AND ITS CREW IN NEW YORK ToList

Making himself as presentable as possible, [21] Talbot reported to Headquarters, and was posted to "J" Company, 4th Battalion. That night he had dinner with them. New men were arriving every few minutes, and the next day, after he had been transferred to "K" Company, they continued to arrive. The nucleus of this company were officers of the original tanks, three or four of them perhaps, and the rest was made up with the newcomers.

Men continued to arrive in driblets, from the beginning of December to the first of January. When a new man joins an old regiment there is a reserve about the others which is rather chilling. They wait to see whether he is going to fit in, before they make any attempts to fit him in. In a way, this very aloofness makes for comfort on the part of the newcomer. At mess, he is left alone until he is absorbed naturally. It gives him a chance to find his level.

All this was different with the Tank Corps. With the exception of the very few officers who were "old men," we were all painfully new, so that we regarded one another without criticism and came to know each other without having [22] to break through the wall of reserve and instinctive mistrust which is characteristically British. A happy bond of good-fellowship was formed immediately.

The first few days were spent in finding billets for the men. They were finally quartered at a hospice in the village. This was a private almshouse, in charge of a group of French nuns, where lived a number of old men and women, most of them in the last stages of consumption. The Hospice consisted of the old Abbey of Ste. Berthe, built in the twelfth century, and several outbuildings around a courtyard. In these barns lived the men, and one large room was reserved for the officers' mess. The Company Orderly Room and Quartermaster's Stores were also kept in the Hospice, and four or five officers were quartered above the Refectory. The buildings were clean and comfortable, and the only drawback lay in the fact that one sometimes found it objectionable to have to look at these poor old creatures, dragging themselves around. They had nothing to do, it seemed, but to wait and die. One old man [23] was a gruesome sight. He was about ninety years old and spent his days walking about the courtyard, wearing a cigarette tin hung around his neck, into which he used to cough with such terrible effort that it seemed as if he would die every time the spasm shook him. As a matter of fact, he and many others did die before we left the village: the extreme cold was too much for them; or perhaps it was the fact that their quiet had been invaded by the "mad English."

It was during this time that Talbot developed a positive genius for disappearing whenever a gray habit came into sight. The nuns were splendid women: kind and hospitable and eager for our comfort, but they did not like to be imposed upon, however slightly. The first thing that Frenchwomen do—and these nuns were no exception—when soldiers are billeted with them, is to learn who is the officer in charge, in order that they may lose no time in bringing their complaints to him. The Mother Superior of the Hospice selected Talbot with unerring zeal. His days were made miserable, until in self-defence he thought of formulating [24] a new calendar of "crimes" for his men, in which would be included all the terrible offences which the Mother Superior told off to him.

Did the Colonel send for Captain Talbot, and did Talbot hurry off to obey the command, just so surely would the Mother Superior select that moment to bar his path.

"Ah, mon Capitaine!" she would exclaim, with a beaming smile. "J'ai quelque chose à vous dire. Un soldat—"

Talbot would break in politely, just as she had settled down for a good long chat, and explain that the Colonel wished to see him. As well try to move the Rock. It was either stand and listen, or go into the presence of his superior officer with an excited nun following him with tales of the "crimes" his men had committed. Needless to say, the Mother Superior conquered. Talbot would have visions of some fairly serious offence, and would hear the tale of a soldier who had borrowed a bucket an hour ago, promising, on his honour as a soldier of the King, to return it in fifty minutes at the most.

"And it is now a full sixty minutes by the [25] clock on the kitchen mantel, M'sieu le Capitaine," she would say, her colour mounting, "and your soldier has not returned my bucket. If he does not bring it back, when can we get another bucket?"

And so on, until Talbot would pacify her, promising her that the bucket would be returned. Then he would go on to the Colonel, breathless and perturbed, his mind so full of buckets that there was hardly room for the business of the Tank Corps. Small wonder that the sight of a gray habit was enough to unnerve the man.

He, himself, was billeted with a French family, just around the corner from the Hospice. The head of the family had been, in the halcyon days before the war, the village butcher. There was now Madame, the little Marie, a sturdy boy about twelve, and the old Grand'mère. The husband was away, of course,—"dans les tranchées," explained Madame with copious tears.

Talbot was moved to sympathy, and made a few tactful inquiries as to where the husband was now, and how he had fared.

[26] "Il est maintenant à Paris," said Madame with a sigh.

"In Paris! What rank has he?—a General, maybe?"

"Ah, M'sieu s'amuse," said Madame, brightening up. No, her husband was a chef at an officers' mess in Paris, she explained proudly.

He had been there since the war broke out. He would soon come home, the Saints be praised. Then the Captain would hear him tell his tales of life in the Army!

The hero came home one day, and great was the rejoicing. Thrilling evenings the family spent around the stove while they listened to stories of great deeds. On the day when his *permission* was finished, and he set out for his hazardous post once more, great was the lamenting. Madame wept. All the brave man's relatives poured in to kiss him good-bye. The departing soldier wept, himself. Even Grand'mère desisted for that day from cracking jokes, which she was always doing in a patois that to Talbot was unintelligible.

But they were very kind to Talbot, and [27] very courageous through the hard winter. When he lay ill with fever in his little low room, where the frost whitened the plaster and icicles hung from the ceiling, Madame and all the others were most solicitous for his comfort. His appreciation and thanks were sincere.

By the middle of December the Battalion had finally settled down and we began our training. Our first course of study was in the mechanism of the tanks. We marched down, early one morning, to an engine hangar that was both cold and draughty. We did not look in the least like embryo heroes. Over our khaki we wore ill-fitting blue garments which men on the railways, who wear them, call "boilers." The effect of wearing them was to cause us to slouch along, and suddenly Talbot burst out laughing at the spectacle. Then he remembered having heard that some of the original "Tankers" had, during the Somme battles, been mistaken for Germans in their blue dungarees. They had been fired on from some distance away, by their own infantry; though nothing fatal ensued. In consequence, [28] before the next "show" chocolate ones were issued.

In the shadows of the engine shed, a gray armour-plated hulk loomed up.

"There it is!" cried Gould, and started forward for a better look at the "Willie."

Across the face of Rigden, the instructor, flashed a look of scorn and pain. Just such a look you may have seen on the face of a young mother when you refer to her baby as "it."

"Don't call a tank 'it,' Gould," he said with admirable patience. "A tank is either 'he' or 'she'; there is no 'it.'"

"In Heaven's name, what's the difference?" asked Gould, completely mystified. The rest of us were all ears.

"The female tank carries machine guns only," Rigden explained. "The male tank carries light field guns as well as machine guns. Don't ever make the mistake again, any of you fellows."

Having firmly fixed in our minds the fact that we were to begin on a female "Willie," the instruction proceeded rapidly. Rigden opened [29] a little door in the side of the tank. It was about as big as the door to a large, old-fashioned brick oven built into the chimney beside the fireplace. His head disappeared and his body followed after. He was swallowed up, save for a hand that waved to us and a muffled voice which said, "Come on in, you fellows."

Gould went first. He scrambled in, was lost to sight, and then we heard his voice.

McKnutt's infectious laugh rose above the sound of our mirth. But not for long.

"Hurry up!" called Rigden. "You next, McKnutt."

McKnutt disappeared. Then to our further astonishment his rich Irish voice could be heard upraised in picturesque malediction. What was Rigden doing to them inside the tank to provoke such profanity from them both? The rest of us scrambled to find out. We soon learned.

When you enter a tank, you go in head first, entering by the side doors. (There is an emergency exit—a hole in the roof which is used by the wise ones.) You wiggle your body in [30] with more or less grace, and then you stand up. Then, if it is the first time, you are usually profane. For you have banged your head most unmercifully against the steel roof and you learn, once and for all, that it is impossible to stand upright in a tank. Each one of us received our baptism in this way. Seven of us, crouched in uncomfortable positions, ruefully rubbed our heads, to Rigden's intense enjoyment. Our life in a tank had begun!

We looked around the little chamber with eager curiosity. Our first thought was that seven men and an officer could never do any work in such a little place. Eight of us were, at present, jammed in here, but we were standing still. When it came to going into action and moving around inside the tank, it would be impossible, — there was no room to pass one another. So we thought. In front are two stiff seats, one for the officer and one for the driver. Two narrow slits serve as portholes through which to look ahead. In front of the officer is a map board, and gun mounting. Behind the engine, one on each side, are the secondary [31] gears. Down the middle of the tank is the powerful petrol engine, part of it covered with a hood, and along either side a narrow passage through which a man can slide from the officer's and driver's seat back and forth to the mechanism at the rear. There are four gun turrets, two on each side. There is also a place for a gun in the rear, but this is rarely used, for "Willies" do not often turn tail and flee!

Along the steel walls are numberless ingenious little cupboards for stores, and ammunition cases are stacked high. Every bit of space is utilized. Electric bulbs light the interior. Beside the driver are the engine levers. Behind the engine are the secondary gears, by which the machine is turned in any direction. All action inside is directed by signals, for when the tank moves the noise is such as to drown a man's voice.

All that first day and for many days after, we struggled with the intricacies of the mechanism. Sometimes, Rigden despaired of us. We might just as well go back to our regiments, unless they were so glad to be rid of us that [32] they would refuse. On other days, he beamed with pride, even when Darwin and the Old Bird distinguished themselves by asking foolish questions. "Darwin" is, of course, not his right name. Because he came from South Africa and looked like a baboon, we called him "Baboon." So let evolution evolve the name of "Darwin" for him in these pages. As for the Old Bird, no other name could have suited him so well. He was the craftiest old bird at successfully avoiding work we had ever known, and yet he was one of the best liked men in the Company. He was one of those men who are absolutely essential to a mess because of his never-failing cheer and gaiety. He never did a stroke of work that he could possibly "wangle" out of. A Scotchman by birth, he was about thirty-eight years old and had lived all over the world. He had a special fondness for China. Until he left "K" Company, he was never known by any other name than that of "Old Bird."

There was one man, from another Company, who gave us the greatest amusement during our Tank-mechanism Course. He was [33] pathetically in earnest, but appeared to have no brains at all. Sometimes, while asking each other catch questions, we would put the most senseless ones to him.

Darwin would say, "Look here, how is the radiator connected with the differential?"

The poor fellow would ponder for a minute or two and then reply, "Oh! through the magneto."

He naturally failed again and again to pass his tests, and was returned to his old Corps.

Somehow we learned not to attempt to stand upright in our steel prison. Before long, McKnutt had ceased his remarks about sardines in a tin and announced, "Sure! there is plenty of room and to spare for a dozen others here." The Old Bird no longer compared the atmosphere, when we were all shut in tight, with the Black Hole of Calcutta. In a word, we had succumbed to the "Willies," and would permit no man to utter a word of criticism against them.

It is necessary here, perhaps, to explain why we always call our machines "Willies." When [34] the tanks were first being experimented upon, they evolved two, a big and a little one. Standing together they looked so ludicrous, that they were nicknamed "Big" and "Little Willie." The name stuck; and now, no one in the Corps refers to his machine in any other way.

A few days before Christmas, our tank course was finished, and the Old Bird suggested a celebration. McKnutt led the cheering. Talbot had an idea.

"Let's get a box-body and go over to Amiens and do our Christmas shopping," he said.

A chorus of "Jove, that's great!" arose. Every one made himself useful excepting the Old Bird, who made up by contributing more than any one else to the gaiety of the occasion. The car was secured, and we all piled in, making early morning hideous with our songs.

We sped along over the snowy roads. War seemed very far away. We were extraordinarily light-hearted. After about twenty miles the cold sobered us down a little. Suddenly, the car seemed to slip from under us and we found [35] ourselves piled up in the soft snow of the road. A rear wheel had shot off, and it went rolling along on its own. Fortunately we had been going rather slowly since we were entering a town, and no one was hurt. Borwick, the musician of the Company, looked like a snow image; Darwin and the Old Bird were locked in each other's arms, and had an impromptu and friendly wrestling match in a snowdrift. McKnutt was invoking the aid of the Saints in his endeavours to prevent the snow from trickling down his back. Talbot and Gould, who had got off lightly, supplied the laughter. The wheel was finally rescued and restored to its proper place, and we crawled along at an ignominious pace until the spires of Amiens welcomed us.

We shopped in the afternoon, buying all sorts of ridiculous things, and collecting enough stores to see us through a siege. After a hilarious dinner at the Hôtel de l'Univers (never had the Old Bird been so witty and gay), we started back about eleven o'clock, and forgetting our injured wheel, raced out of the town [36] toward home. A short distance down the main boulevard, the wheel again came off, and this time the damage could not be repaired. There was nothing for it but to wait until morning, and it was a disconsolate group that wandered about. All the hotels were full up. Finally, a Y.M.C.A. hut made some of us welcome. We sat about, reading and talking, until we dozed off in our chairs. The next morning we got a new wheel and ran gingerly the sixty-odd miles back, to regale the others with enviable tales of our pre-Christmas festivities.

[37]

III

**LATER DAYS OF TRAINING **

"Well, thank Heaven, that sweat's over," said the Old Bird the night after we finished our tank course, and had our celebration. He stretched luxuriously.

"Yes, but you're starting off again on the gun to-morrow morning," said the Major, cheerfully.

The Old Bird protested.

"But I can have a few days' rest, sir, can't I?" he said sorrowfully.

The Major laughed.

"No, you can't. You're down, so you'll have to go through with it."

So for three days we sat in the open, in the driving sleet, from half-past eight in the morning until half-past four in the afternoon, learning the gun. On the fourth day we finished off our course with firing on the range. Surprising as it may seem, after two or three rounds [38] we could hit the very smallest object at a distance of four or five hundred yards.

"How many more courses must we go through?" asked the Old Bird of Rigden, as they strolled back one evening from the range. The Old Bird was always interested in how much—or, rather, how little—work he had before him.

"There's the machine gun; the signalling course,—you'll have to work hard on that, but I know you don't object,—and also revolver practice. Aren't you thrilled?"

"No, I'm not," grumbled the Old Bird. "Life isn't worth living with all this work to do. I wish we could get into action."

"So do I," said Talbot, joining them. "But while we're waiting, wouldn't you rather be back here with good warm billets and a comfortable bed and plenty to eat, instead of sitting in a wet trench with the Infantry?" He remembered an old man in his regiment who had been with the Salvation Army at home. He would stump along on his flat feet, trudging miles with his pack on his back, and [39] Talbot had never heard him complain. He was bad at drill. He could never get the orders or formations through his head. Talbot had often lost patience with him, but the old fellow was always cheerful. One morning, in front of Bapaume, after a night of terrible cold, the old man could not move. Talbot tried to cheer him up and to help him, but he said feebly: "I think I'm done for—I don't believe I shall ever get warm. But never mind, sir." And in a few minutes he died, as uncomplainingly as he had lived.

"You're right, of course, Talbot," the Old Bird said. "We're very well off here. But, I say, how I should like to be down in Boulogne for a few days!" And until they reached the Mess, the Old Bird dilated on the charm of Boulogne and all the luxuries he would indulge in the next time he visited the city.

The rest of that week found us each day parading at eight o'clock in the courtyard of the Hospice, and after instruction the various parties marched off to their several duties. Some of us went to the tankdrome; some of [40] us to the hills overlooking historic Agincourt, and others to the barn by the railroad where we practised with the guns. Another party accompanied Borwick to a secluded spot where he drilled them in machine-gun practice. Borwick was as skilful with a machine gun as with a piano. This was the highest praise one could give him.

That night at mess, Gould said suddenly:—

"To-morrow's a half day, isn't it?"

"Of course. Wake up, you idiot," said Talbot. "We're playing 'J' Company at soccer, and on Sunday we're playing 'L' at rugger. Two strenuous days before us. Are you feeling fit?"

Gould was feeling most awfully fit. In fact, he assured the mess that he, alone, was a match for "J" Company.

Our soccer team was made up almost entirely of men who had been professional players. We had great pride in them, so that on the following afternoon, an eager crowd streamed out of the village to our football field, which we had selected with great care. It [41] was as flat as a cricket pitch. A year ago it had been ploughed as part of the French farmland, and now here were the English playing football!

Before the game began there was a good deal of cheerful chaffing on the respective merits of the "J" and "K" Company teams. And when the play was in progress and savage yells rent the air, the French villagers looked on in wonder and pity. They had always believed the English to be mad. Now they were convinced of it.

From the outset, however, "J" Company was hopelessly out-classed, and wishing to be generous to a failing foe, we ceased our wild cheering. "J" Company, on the other hand, wishing to exhort their team to greater efforts, made up for our moderation, with the result that our allies were firmly convinced that "J" Company had won the game! If not, why should they dance up and down and wave their hats and shriek? And even the score, five to one in favor of "K" Company, failed to convince them entirely. But "K" went home to [42] an hilarious tea, with a sense of work well done.

And what of the rugger game the next day? Let us draw a veil over it. Suffice it to say that the French congratulated "K" Company over the outcome of that, although the score was twelve to three in favor of "J"!

We awoke on Monday morning with a delightful feeling that something pleasant was going to happen, for all the world the same sensation we used to experience on waking on our birthday and suddenly remembering that gifts were sure to appear and that there would be something rather special for tea! By the time full con-sciousness returned, we remembered that this was the day when, for the first time, the tank was to be set in motion. Even the Old Bird was eager.

We hurry off to the tankdrome. One after another we slide in through the little door and are swallowed up. The door is bolted behind the last to enter. Officer and driver slip into their respective seats. The steel shutters of the portholes click as they are opened. The [43] gunners take their positions. The driver opens the throttle a little and tickles the carburetor, and the engine is started up. The driver races the engine a moment, to warm her up. The officer reaches out a hand and signals for first speed on each gear; the driver throws his lever into first; he opens the throttle: the tank—our "Willie"—moves!

Supposing you were locked in a steel box, with neither portholes to look through nor airholes to breathe from. Supposing you felt the steel box begin to move, and, of course, were unable to see where you were going. Can you imagine the sensation? Then you can guess the feelings of the men in a tank,—excepting the officer and driver, who can see ahead through their portholes,—when the monster gets under way. There are times, of course, with the bullets flying thick and fast, when all portholes, for officer, driver, and gunners, must be closed. Then we plunge ahead, taking an occasional glimpse through the special pin-point holes.

Thirty tons of steel rolls along with its [44] human freight. Suddenly, the driver rings a bell. He presses another button, and signals the driver of the right-hand track into "neutral." This disconnects the track from the engine. The tank swings around to the right. The right-hand driver gets the signal "First speed," and we are off again, at a right angle to our former direction.

Now we are headed for a gentle slope across the field, and as we approach it, the tank digs her nose into the base of the hill. She crawls up. The men in the rear tip back and enjoy it hugely. If the hill is steep enough they may even find themselves lying flat on their backs or standing on their heads! But no such luck. Presently they are standing as nearly upright as it is ever possible to stand, and the tank is balancing on the top of the slope. The driver is not expert as yet, and we go over with an awful jolt and tumble forward. This is rare fun!

But the instructor is not pleased. We must try it all over again. So back again to attack the hill a second time. The top is reached once more and we balance there. The driver throws [45] out his clutch, we slip over very gently, and carefully he lets the clutch in again and down we go. The "Willie" flounders around for the fraction of a second. Then, nothing daunted, she starts off once more. We have visions of her sweeping all before her some day far behind the German lines.

Three or four weeks of this sort of thing, and we are hardened to it.

Our reward came at last, however. After mess one morning, when the conversation had consisted mainly of the question, "When are we going into a show?" with no answer to the question, we were called into the Major's room, where he told us, in strictest secrecy, that in about three weeks a big attack was to come off. We should go in at last!

For the next two or three weeks we studied maps and aeroplane photographs, marking out our routes, starting-points, rear ammunition-dumps, forward dumps, and lines of supply. At last, then, our goal loomed up and these months of training, for the most part interesting, but at times terribly boring, would bear [46] fruit. Two direct results were noticeable now on looking back to the time when we joined. First, each man in the Battalion knew how to run a tank, how to effect slight repairs, how to work the guns, and how to obtain the best results from the machine. Second, and very important, was the fact that the men and officers had got together. The crews and officers of each section knew and trusted each other. The strangeness of feeling that was apparent in the first days had now entirely disappeared, and that cohesion of units which is so essential in warfare had been accomplished. Each of us knew the other's faults and the mistakes he was prone to make. More important still, we knew our own faults and weaknesses and had the courage to carry on and overcome them.

A few nights before we moved up the line, we gave a grand concert. Borwick and the Old Bird planned it. On an occasion of this sort, the Old Bird never grumbled at the amount of work he was obliged to do. Some weeks before we had bought a piano from one of the inhabitants of the village, and the piano was [47] naturally the *pièce de résistance* of the concert. The Old Bird went around for days at a time, humming scraps of music with unintelligible words which it afterwards developed at the concert were awfully good songs of his own composing. The Battalion tailor was called in to make up rough Pierrot costumes. The Old Bird drilled us until we begged for mercy, while Borwick strummed untiringly at the piano. At last the great night arrived.

A stage had been built at one end of a hangar, and curtains hung up.

The whole of the Staff and H.Q. had been invited, and the *maire*, the *curé*, the *médecin* of the village, and their families were also to attend.

Promptly at eight o'clock, the concert began, with Borwick at the piano. Everything went off without a hitch. Although "K" Company provided most of the talent, the Battalion shared the honours of the entertainment. Each song had a chorus, and so appreciative was our audience that the choruses were repeated again and again. The one "lady" of [48] the Troupe looked charming, and "she" arranged for "her" voice to be entirely in keeping with "her" dress and paint. The French spectators enjoyed it hugely. They were a great encouragement, for they laughed at everything uproariously, though it could not have been due to their understanding of the jokes.

At ten o'clock we finished off with "God Save the King," and went back to our billets feeling that our stay in the village had been splendidly rounded off.

[49]

IV

MOVING UP THE LINE ToC

Two or three days before we were due to leave, we had received orders to pack our surplus kit, and have it at the Quartermaster's Stores at a certain time. We drew a long breath. This meant that the actual date, which up to the present had been somewhat indefinite, was close at hand. We were given orders to draw our tanks and the whole Company was marched over to work sheds about two miles away at E——, where tanks and stores were issued.

The variety and number of little things which it is necessary to draw when fitting out a tank for action is inconceivable. Tools, small spares, Pyrenes, electric lamps, clocks, binoculars, telescopes, petrol and oil funnels, oil squirts, grease guns, machine guns, headlights, tail lamps, steel hawsers, crowbars, shovels, picks, inspection lamps, and last, but not least, ammunition. The field-gun ammunition has to be taken out [50] of its boxes and placed in the shell racks inside the tank. The S.A.A. (small arms ammunition) must be removed from its boxes and stacked away. At the same time every single round, before being put into the drum, must be gauged. All this has to be done in the last two or three days, and everything must be checked and countersigned. There is always a great deal of fun for Tank Commanders in drawing their stores. It is a temptation, when in the midst of all these thousands of articles, to seize the opportunity, when no one is looking, to pocket a few extra spares and dainty little tools, not, of course, for one's own personal benefit, but simply because such things are always being lost or stolen, and it is exasperating, to say the least, to find one's self, at a critical moment, without some article which it is impossible to duplicate at the time.

During these last few days it was a continual march for the men from B—— to E——. Very often they were called back when their day's work was over to draw some new article or make some alteration which had been [51] forgotten at the time they were in the workshops.

At last, however,—on the third day following the grand concert,—the kits were packed, loaded on to the lorries, and sent off to E——. The troops said "Good-bye" to the village which had been such a happy home and school during that winter of 1916, and the officers made their fond adieus to the mothers and daughters of the houses in which they had been billeted.

The companies formed up and marched along to the workshops. Every one was in high spirits, and there was a friendly race to see which Company of the Battalion could load up their tanks in the shortest time on to the specially constructed steel trucks.

A few days before all these activities commenced, Talbot and another Tank Commander had gone on to the tanks' ultimate destination, A——, a village which had been evacuated a few days before by the Germans on their now famous retirement to the Hindenburg Line. It was a most extraordinary sight to [52] ride along the road from Albert to Bapaume, which during the summer and winter of the preceding year had witnessed such heavy fighting. The whole country on each side of the road was a desolate vista of shell-holes as far as the eye could see. Where villages had been, there was now no trace left of any sort of habitation. One might think that, however heavy a bombardment, some trace would be left of the village which had suffered. There was literally nothing left of the village through which had run the road they were now travelling. Over this scarred stretch of country were dotted camps and groups of huts, with duck-boards crossing the old shell-holes, some of which were still full of water.

On approaching B—— they saw traces everywhere of the methodical and organized methods by which the Germans had retired. The first sign was a huge shell-crater in the middle of the road, about forty feet deep, which the Boche had arranged to prevent armoured cars from following him up. If they did succeed, the transports would be delayed in [53] reaching them, at all events. These holes were rather a nuisance, for the road itself was a mass of lesser shell-craters and the soft ground on each side was impassable. The road was crowded with engineers and labor battalions, filling in the shell-holes, and laying railways into the outskirts of A——.

In A—— the old German notices were still standing as they had been left. Strung across the road on a wire was a notice which read: "Fuhrweg nach Behagnies." Every house in the town had been pulled down. The wily Boche had not even blown them up. Instead he had saved explosives by attaching steel hawsers to the houses and by means of tractors had pulled them down, so that the roof and sides fell in on the foundation. Every pump handle in the village had been broken off short, and not a single piece of furniture was left behind. Later, we found the furniture from this and other villages in the Hindenburg Line.

Saddest of all, however, was the destruction of the beautiful poplar trees which once bordered the long French roads built by Napoleon. [54] These had been sawn off at their base and allowed to fall on the side of the road, not across it, as one might suppose. If they had been allowed to fall across the road, the Boche, himself, would have been hindered in his last preparations for his retreat. Everything was done with military ends in view. The villages were left in such a condition as to make them uninhabitable, the more to add to our discomfort and to make our hardships severer. The trees were cut down only on those parts of the road which were screened from observation from his balloons and present trenches. In some places where the road dipped into a valley the trees had been left untouched.

At the place where our tanks were scheduled to arrive, and which had lately been a railhead of the Boche, all the metals had been torn up, and in order to destroy the station itself, he had smashed the cast-iron pillars which supported the roof, and in consequence the whole building had fallen in. But nothing daunted, the British engineers were even now working at top speed laying down new lines. Some of the [55] metals, which a few short weeks before had been lying in countless stacks down on the quays at the Bases, now unrolled themselves at the rate of about two and a quarter miles a day. One interesting feature of this rapid track-laying was that when the tank train left E——, on its two and a half days' journey down to the railhead at A——, the track on which the train was to run was not completed into A— —. But, nevertheless, the track arrived ahead of the train, which was the main point!

As they rode into the ruined village of A— — Talbot and his companion came across still further evidence of the steps which the German will take to inconvenience his enemy. In order to battle against the hordes of rats which are so prevalent in the old parts of the line in France, the Boche breeds cats in enormous numbers. Yet, in order to carry out to the limit his idea that nothing of value should fall into our hands, he had killed every cat in the village. In every house three or four of these poor little creatures lay around with their heads chopped off. Tabby cats, black cats, white cats, and little [56] kittens, all dead. Farther on, over a well at the corner of the main square was posted a sign which read: "This well is poisoned. Do not touch. By order. R.E."

Here and there a house had been left intact, with its furniture untouched. It was not until later that it struck us as peculiar that these houses had been spared from the general destruction. Two or three days later, however, after we had moved in, and headquarters had been established, we discovered that under many of these houses, and at certain crossroads which had not been blown up in the usual manner, the Boche had left mines, timed to go off at any time up to twenty-eight days. One could never be sure that the ground underneath one's feet would not blow up at any moment. These mines were small boxes of high explosive, inside of which was a little metal tube with trigger and detonator attached. Inside the tube was a powerful acid, which, when it had eaten its way through, set free the trigger and exploded the charge. The length of time it took for the mine to explode was gauged [57] by the strength or weakness of the acid in the tube.

We were also impressed with the mechanical genius of the German. The Boche had made a veritable mechanical toy out of nearly every house in the village which he had spared. Delightful little surprises had been prepared for us everywhere. Kick a harmless piece of wood, and in a few seconds a bomb exploded. Pick up a bit of string from the floor and another bomb went off. Soon we learned to be wary of the most innocent objects. Before touching anything we made elaborate preparations for our safety.

One of the men was greatly annoyed by a wire which hung over his head when he was asleep, but he did not wish to remove it. He had decided that it was connected with some devilish device which would do him no good. Finally, one morning, he could endure this sword of Damocles no longer. With two boon companions, he carefully attached a string about fifteen yards long to the wire. They tiptoed gently out of the house to a discreet distance, [58] and with a yell of triumph, the hero pulled the string, — and nothing happened!

But there was another side to all this. McKnutt some time afterwards came in with an interesting story. Some Sappers, he said, had been digging under a house in the village, presumably for the mysterious reasons that always drive the Engineers to dig in unlikely places. One of them pushed his shovel into what had been the cellar of the house, but as the roof had fallen in on the entrance, they did not know of its existence. When they finally forced their way in, they found two German officers and two Frenchwomen in a terribly emaciated condition. One of the Boches and one of the women lay dead, locked in each other's arms. The other two still breathed, but when they were brought up into the open they expired within a few hours without either of them giving an explanation. The only reason we could find for their terrible plight was that the women had been forced down there by the officers to undergo a last farewell, while the Germans were destroying the village, and that the house had [59] fallen in on top of them. Later, probably no one knew where they had disappeared, and they were unable to get out of the ruins or to make themselves heard. The village of A — — gained a romantic reputation after that, and it was curious to realize that we had been living there for days while this silent tragedy was being enacted.

In addition to the destruction in the towns, the beautiful orchards which are so numerous in France were ruined. Apple, pear, and plum trees lay uprooted on the ground, and here again the military mind of the German had been at work. He did not wish the fruit that the trees would bear in future to fall into our hands.

But although the village was a pretty poor place in which to stay, the near presence of a B.E.F. Canteen was a comfort. It is always amazing to visit one of these places. Within perhaps four or five miles of the firing line we have stores selling everything from a silver cigarette case to a pair of boots, and everything, too, at nearly cost price. The Canteen [60] provides almost every variety of smoking materials, and eatables, and their only disadvantage is that they make packages from home seem so useless. As the tobaccos come straight out of bond, it is far cheaper to buy them at the Canteen, than to have them forwarded from home. These Canteens are managed by the Army, and are dotted all over the country inhabited by the British troops. Since they have sprung into existence life at the front has been far more comfortable and satisfactory in France, and people at home are discovering that money is the best thing to send out to their men.

Finally, one cold, sunny morning, about half-past five, the tank train steamed slowly into A — —, and drew up on a siding. It was not possible to begin the work of unloading the tanks until night fell. So the tired crews turned into the roofless houses which had been prepared for them, and slept until dusk. When darkness fell, as if by magic, the town sprang to activity.

[61]

V

PREPARATIONS FOR THE SHOW

That night the engines were started up, and one by one the tanks crawled off the train. Although the day had begun with brilliant sunshine, at dusk the snow had begun to fall, and by the time the tanks came off, the snow was a foot thick on the ground. The tanks moved down to the temporary tankdrome which had been decided upon near the railway, and the sponson trucks were towed there. The night was spent in fitting on the sponsons to the sides of the machines. It was bitterly cold. The sleet drove in upon us all night, stinging our hands and faces. Everything seemed to go wrong. We had the utmost difficulty in making the bolt-holes fit, and as each sponson weighs about three tons they were not easy to move and adjust. We drove ahead with the work, knowing that it must be done while the darkness lasted.

[62] Finally, about two hours before dawn broke, the last bolt was fastened, and the tanks were ready to move. The night was blacker than ever as they lumbered out of the tankdrome, and were led across the snow to a halfway house about four miles from the rail-head, and an equal distance from the front-line trenches. We had not quite reached our destination when the darkness began to lift in the east, and with feverish energy we pushed ahead, through the driving snow.

Late that afternoon, Talbot was again sent ahead with five or six troopers and orderlies to a village in the front line. It was necessary for us to spend three or four days there before the attack commenced, in order to study out the vulnerable points in the German line. We were to decide also the best routes for the tanks to take in coming up to the line, and those to be taken later in crossing No Man's Land when the "show" was on. We rode along across fields denuded of all their trees. The country here was utterly unlike that to which we had been accustomed in "peace-time trench [63] warfare." This last expression sounds like an anomaly, but actually it means the life which is led in trenches where one may go along for two or three months without attacking. In comparison with our existence when we are making an offensive, the former seems like life in peace times. Hence, the expression. But from this it must not be supposed that "peace-time trench warfare" is all beer and skittles. Quite the contrary. As a matter of fact, during four or five days in the trenches there may be as many casualties as during an attack, but taking it on an average, naturally the losses and dangers are greater when troops go over the top. Curiously enough, too, after one has been in an attack the front-line trench seems a haven of refuge. Gould, who was wounded in the leg during a battle on the Somme, crawled into a shell-hole. It was a blessed relief to be lying there, even though the bullets were whistling overhead. At first he felt no pain, and he wished, vaguely, that he had brought a magazine along to read! All through the burning summer day he stayed there, [64] waiting for the night. As soon as it was dark he wriggled back to our trenches, tumbled over the parapet of the front-line trench, and narrowly escaped falling on the point of a bayonet. But he never forgets the feeling of perfect safety and peace at being back, even in an exposed trench, with friends.

The fields across which we rode had been ploughed the preceding autumn by the French civilians. Later, when the snow had disappeared, we could see where the ground had been torn up by the horses of a German riding-school of ten days before. On some of the roads the ruts and heavy marks of the retreating German transports could still be seen. It was a new and exciting experience to ride along a road which only two or three days before had been traversed by the Germans in a retreat, even though they called it a "retirement." The thought was very pleasant to men who, for the last two years, had been sitting *in front* of the Boche month after month, and who, even in an attack, had been unable to find traces of foot, hoof, or wheel mark because of [65] the all-effacing shell-fire. Here and there were places where the Boche had had his watering-troughs, and also the traces of scattered huts and tents on the ground where the grass, of a yellowish green, still showed. The front line of defence here was really no front line at all, but was merely held as in open warfare by outposts, sentry groups, and patrols.

At night it was the easiest thing in the world to lose one's self close up to the line and wander into the German trenches. In fact, over the whole of this country, where every landmark had been destroyed and where owing to the weather the roads were little different from the soil on each side, a man could lose himself and find no person or any sign to give him his direction. The usual guide which one might derive from the Verey lights going up between the lines was here non-existent, as both sides kept extremely quiet. Even the guns were comparatively noiseless in these days, and were a man to find himself at night alone upon this ground, which lay between two and three miles behind our own lines, the only thing he [66] could do would be to lie down and wait for the dawn to show him the direction.

As we rode toward O— — our only guide was a few white houses two or three miles away on the edge of the village. The German had not evacuated O— — of his own free will, but a certain "Fighting Division" had taken the village two days before and driven the German out, when he retired three or four hundred yards farther to his rear Hindenburg Line. The probable reason why he hung on to this village, which was really in front of his line of advance, was because at the time he decided to retire on the Somme, the Hindenburg Line was incomplete. In fact, the Boche could still be seen working on his wire and trenches.

We arrived in O— — at nightfall. Some batteries were behind the village, and the Germans were giving the village and the guns a rather nasty time. Unhappily for us, the Boche artillery were dropping five-nine's on the road which led into the village, and as they seemed unlikely to desist, we decided to make a dash [67] for it. The horses were a bit nervous, but behaving very well under the trying circumstances. (With us were some limbers bringing up ammunition.) Shells were exploding all around us. It would never do to stand still.

The dash up that hundred yards of road was an unpleasant experience. As we made the rush, the gunners tearing along "hell for leather" and the others galloping ahead on their plunging horses, we heard the dull whistle and the nearer roar of two shells approaching. Instinctively we leaned forward. We held our breath.

When a shell drops near, there is always the feeling that it is going to fall on one's head. We flattened ourselves out and urged our horses to greater speed. The shells exploded about thirty yards behind us, killing two gunners and their mules, while the rest of us scrambled into the village and under cover.

In the darkness, we found what had once been the shop of the village blacksmith, and in the forge we tied up our horses. It was bitterly cold. It was either make a fire and trust to luck that it would not be observed, or freeze. [68] We decided on the fire, and in its grateful warmth we lay down to snatch the first hours of sleep we had had in nearly three days. But the German gunners were most inconsiderate, and a short time afterward they dropped a small barrage down the road. The front of our forge was open, and we were obliged to flatten ourselves on the ground to prevent the flying splinters from hitting us. When this diversion was over, we stirred up our fire, and made some tea, just in time to offer some to a gunner sergeant who came riding up. He hitched his horse to one of the posts, and sat down with us by the fire. The shell-fire had quieted down, and we dozed off, glad of the interlude. Suddenly a shell burst close beside us. The poor beast, waiting patiently for his rider, was hit in the neck by the shrapnel, but hardly a sound escaped him. In war, especially, one cannot help admiring the stoicism of horses, as compared with other animals. One sees examples of it on all sides. Tread, for instance, on a dog's foot, and he runs away, squealing. A horse is struck by a large lump of shrapnel [69] just under its withers, and the poor brute trembles, but makes no sound. Almost the only time that horses scream—and the sound is horrible—is when they are dying. Then they shriek from sheer pain and fear. Strange as it may seem, one is often more affected by seeing horses struck than when men are killed. Somehow they seem so particularly helpless.

It was during these days at O— — that Talbot discovered Johnson. Johnson was one of his orderlies. Although it did not lie in the path of his duty, he took the greatest delight in doing all sorts of little odd jobs for Talbot. So unobtrusive he was about it all, that for some time Talbot hardly noticed that some one was trying to make him comfortable. When he did, by mutual agreement Johnson became his servant and faithful follower through everything. The man was perfectly casual and apparently unaffected by the heaviest shell-fire. It is absurd to say that a man "doesn't mind shell-fire." Every one dislikes it, and gets nervous under it. The man who "doesn't mind it" is the man who fights [70] his nervousness and gets such control of himself that he is able to *appear* as if he were unaffected. Between "not minding it" and "appearing not to mind it" lie hard-won moral battles, increased strength of character, and victory over fear. Johnson had accomplished this. He preserved an attitude of careless calm, and could walk down a road with shells bursting all around him with a sublime indifference that was inspiring. Between him and his officer sprang up an extraordinary and lasting affection.

The wretched night in the forge at last came to an end, and the next morning we looked around for more comfortable billets. We selected the cellar of a house in fairly good condition and prepared to move in, when we discovered that we were not the first to whom it had appealed. Two dead Germans still occupied the premises, and when we had disposed of the bodies, we took up our residence. Here we stayed, going out each day to find the best points from which to view No Man's Land, which lay in front of the village. With the aid [71] of maps, we planned the best routes for the tanks to take when the battle should have begun. Not a detail was neglected.

Then something happened to break the monotony of life. Just back of the village one of our batteries was concealed in such a fashion that it was impossible to find it from an aeroplane. Yet every day, regularly, the battery was shelled. Every night under cover of the darkness, the position was changed, and the battery concealed as cleverly as before, but to no avail. The only solution was that some one behind our lines was in communication with the Germans, *every day*. Secrecy was increased. Guards were doubled to see that no one slipped through the lines. Signals were watched. The whole affair was baffling, and yet we could find no clue.

Just in front of the wood where the battery was concealed, stood an old farmhouse where a genial Frenchwoman lived and dispensed good cheer to us. She had none of the men of her own family nor any farmhands to help her, but kept up the farmwork all alone. Every day, usually [72] in the middle of the morning, she went out to the fields behind her house and ploughed, with an old white horse drawing the plough. For some reason she never ploughed more than one or two furrows at a time, and when this was done, she drove the white horse back to the barn. One day, an officer noticed that a German plane hovered over the field while the woman was ploughing, and that when she went back to the house, the plane shot away. The next day the same thing happened. Later in the day, the battery received its daily reminder from the Boche gunners, as unerringly accurate as ever.

Here was a clue. The solution of the problem followed. The woman knew the position of the battery, and every day when she went out to plough, she drove the white horse up and down, making a furrow directly in front of the battery. When the men in the German plane saw the white horse, they flew overhead, took a photograph of the newly turned furrow, and turned the photograph over to their gunners. The rest was easy.

A TANK GOING OVER A TRENCH ON ITS WAY INTO ACTION ToList

[73] The next day we missed three events which had become part of our daily life. The German plane no longer hovered in the air. Our battery, for the first time in weeks, spent a peaceful day. And in

the field behind her house, a woman with an old white horse no longer made the earth ready for the sowing.

For three days now we had received no rations, and were obliged to subsist on the food which the Boche had left behind him when he fled. Finally, when all our plans were complete, we were notified that the point of attack had been shifted to N— —, a village about four miles away. This practical joke we thought in extremely bad taste, but there was nothing for it but to pack up and move as quickly as possible. We learned that our troops at N— — had tried twice to break through the German lines by bombing. A third attempt was to be made, and the tanks were depended upon to open the way. Hence the change in our plans.

Early the next morning we left O— —, and dashed along a road which lay parallel with our [74] line, and was under direct observation from the German trenches. Owing to the fact, probably, that he was not properly settled in his new line, the Boche did not bother us much, excepting at one place, where we were obliged to make a run for it. We arrived at N— — just after the tanks had been brought up. They were hurricdly concealed close up to houses, in cuttings, and under trees.

The show was scheduled to come off the next morning at 4.30. That night we gathered at Brigade Headquarters and made the final plans. Each tank had its objective allotted to it, and marked out on the Tank Commander's course. Each tank was to go just so far and no farther. Talbot and Darwin were detailed to go forward as far as possible on foot when the battle was in progress, and send back messages as to how the show was progressing. Talbot also was given the task of going out that night to make the marks in No Man's Land which would guide the tanks in the morning.

At eleven o'clock, in the bright moonlight, Talbot, with Johnson and a couple of orderlies, [75] started out. They climbed over the front line, which was at present a railway embankment, crawled into No Man's Land, and set to work. Immediately the Boche snipers spotted them and bullets began to whistle over their heads.

Luckily, no one was hit, but a couple of "whizz bangs" dropped uncomfortably close. The men dropped for cover. Only Johnson stood still, his figure black against the white snow gleaming in the moonlight.

The shells continued to fall about them as they wriggled back when the work was done. As they reached N— — the tanks were being led up toward the line, so that later, under cover of the darkness, they might be taken farther forward to their starting-points.

[76]

VI

THE FIRST BATTLE ToC

At dawn the next morning, the tanks were already lined up, sullen and menacing in the cold half-light. The men shivered in the biting air. One by one the crews entered the machines, and one by one the little steel doors closed behind them. The engines throbbed, and they moved off sluggishly.

Darwin and Talbot, with their orderlies, waited impatiently. The moments just before an attack are always the hardest. A few batteries were keeping up a desultory fire. They glanced at their watches.

"Only a minute to go," said Darwin. "I bet the show's put off or something. Isn't this snow damnably cold, though!"

Suddenly a sixty-pounder in our rear crashed out. Then from all sides a deafening roar burst forth and the barrage began. As we became accustomed to the intensity and [77] ear-splittingness of the sound, the bark of the eighteen-pounders could be faintly distinguished above the dull roar of the eight-inches. The sky-line was lit up with thousands of flashes, large and small, each one showing, for a second, trenches or trees or houses, and during this tornado we knew that the "Willies" must have started forward on their errand.

As the barrage lifted and the noise died down a little, the first streaks of light began to show in the sky, although we could distinguish nothing. No sign of the infantry or of the tanks could be seen. But the ominous sound of machine guns and heavy rifle-fire told us that the Boche was prepared.

We could stand this inactivity no longer. We trudged forward through the snow, taking the broad bands left by the tracks of the busses as our guide, the officers leading the way and the orderlies behind in single file.

"The blighter's starting, himself, now," said Talbot, as a four-two landed a hundred yards away, and pieces of earth came showering down on our heads. Then another and another fell, [78] each closer than the one before, and instinctively we quickened our steps, for it is difficult to walk slowly through shell-fire.

The embankment loomed before us, and big splotches of black and yellow leaped from its surface. The deafening crashes gave us that peculiar feeling in the stomach which danger alone can produce. We scrambled up the crumbling, slaggy sides, and found when we reached the top that the sound of the machine guns had died away, excepting on the extreme left in front of B——, where the ordinary tap of ones and twos had developed into a sharp crackle of tens and twenties. By listening carefully one could feel, rather than hear, the more intermittent bursts from the rifles.

"There's one, sir," shouted one of the orderlies.

"Where?"

"Half-right and about five hundred yards ahead."

By dint of straining, we discovered a little animal—or so it looked—crawling forward on the far side of the Hindenburg Line. Already [79] it was doing a left incline in accordance with its instructions, so as to enfilade a communication trench which ran back to N——. The German observer had spotted her. Here and there, on each side of her, a column of dirt and snow rose into the air. But the little animal seemed to bear a charmed life. No harm came to her, and she went calmly on her way, for all the world like a giant tortoise at which one vainly throws clods of earth.

As it grows lighter, we can now see others in the distance. One is not moving—is it out of action? The only motion on the whole landscape is that of the bursting shells, and the tanks. Over the white snow in front of the German wire, are dotted little black lumps. Some crawl, some move a leg or an arm, and some lie quite still. One who has never seen a modern battle doubtless forms a picture of masses of troops moving forward in splendid formation, with cheering voices and gleaming bayonets. This is quite erroneous. To an observer in a post or in a balloon, no concerted action is visible at all. Here and there a line or [80] two of men dash forward and disappear. A single man or a small group of men wriggle across the ground. That is all.

"Well, they haven't got it in the neck as I supposed," said Darwin. "Remarkably few lying about. Let's push on."

"All right," Talbot assented. "If you like."

We crawled over the top of the embankment and continued down the side. About two hundred yards to the left, we saw one of the tanks, with her nose in the air. A little group of three or four men were digging around her, frantically. We rushed over to them, and found that the Old Bird's 'bus had failed to get over a large pit which lay in the middle of No Man's Land, and was stuck with her tail in the bottom of the ditch. Here occurred one of those extraordinary instances of luck which one notices everywhere in a modern battle. The tank had been there about ten minutes when the German gunners had bracketed on her, and were dropping five-nines, all of them within a radius of seventy yards of the tank, and yet no one was hurt. Finally, by dint of strenuous digging, she [81] started up and pulled herself wearily out of the pit.

A TANK HALFWAY OVER THE TOP AND AWAITING THE ORDER TO ADVANCE IN THE BATTLE OF MENIN ROAD ToList

Suddenly, Darwin shouted:—

"Look here, you fellows! What are these Boches doing?"

Looking up, we saw about forty or fifty Germans stumbling over their own wire, and running toward us as hard as they could go. For a moment we thought it was the preliminary step of a counter-attack, but suddenly we discovered that they carried no arms and were attempting to run with their hands above their heads. At the same time something occurred which is always one of the saddest sights in war. One hears a great deal about the "horrors of war" and the "horrors" of seeing men killed on either side of one, but at the time there is very little "horror" to it. One simply doesn't have time to pay any attention to it all. But the sad part was that the German machine gunners, seeing their men surrendering, opened a furious fire on them. There they were, caught from behind, and many of them dropped from the bullets of their own comrades.

[82] Twenty or thirty of them came straight on, rushed up to the pit where the tank had come to grief, and tumbled down into this refuge. Evidently, they knew of the British passion for souvenirs, for when our men surrounded them, the Germans plucked wildly at their own shoulder straps as if to entreat their captors to take the shoulder straps instead of anything else!

We gave two or three of the wounded Germans some cigarettes and a drink of water. They were then told to find their quickest way to the rear. Like other German prisoners we had seen, they went willingly enough. German discipline obtains even after a man has been made a prisoner. He obeys his captors with the same docility with which he had previously obeyed his own officers. Left to themselves, and started on the right road, the prisoner will plod along, their N.C.O.'s saluting the English officers, and inquiring the way to the concentration camp. When they find it, they usually appear well pleased.

The Old Bird's tank moved on.

[83] "I suppose everything's going all right," said Talbot. "Suppose we move on and see if we can get some information."

"Yes, or some souvenirs," Darwin replied with a laugh.

We pushed on slowly. Three tanks which had completed their job were coming back and passed us. A little later we met some fellows who were slightly wounded and asked them how the battle was going. Every story was different. The wounded are rarely able to give a correct version of any engagement, and we saw that no accurate information was to be gleaned from these men.

We had been out now for an hour and a half and still had no news to send back to Headquarters. We knew how hard it was for the officers behind the lines, who had planned the whole show, to sit hour after hour waiting for news of their troops. The minutes are like hours.

"My God, Darwin, look!" Talbot cried. "Something's happened to her. She's on fire!"

In the distance we saw one of our tanks stuck in the German wire, which at that point [84] was about a hundred yards thick. Smoke was belching from every porthole. A shell had registered a direct hit, exploding the petrol, and the tank was on fire. We dashed forward toward her.

A German machine gun rattled viciously. They had seen us. An instant later, the bullets were spattering around us, and we dropped flat. One man slumped heavily and lay quite still. By inches we crawled forward, nearer and nearer to the blazing monster. Another machine gun snarled at us, and we slid into a shell-hole for protection. Then, after a moment's breathing space, we popped out and tried to rush again. Another man stopped a bullet.

It was suicide to go farther. Into another shell-hole we fell, and thought things over. We decided to send a message, giving roughly the news that the Hindenburg Line and N— — had been taken. An orderly was given a message. He crawled out of the shell-hole, ran a few steps, dropped flat, wriggled along across the snow, sprang to his feet, ran another few steps, and so on until we lost sight of him.

A moment or two later we started across the [85] snow in a direction parallel with the lines. Behind an embankment we came across a little group of Australians at an impromptu dressing-station. Some of them were wounded and the others were binding up their wounds. We watched them for a while and started on again. We had gone about fifty yards when a shell screeched overhead. We turned and saw it land in the middle of the group we had just left. Another shell burst close to us and huge clods of earth struck us in the face and in the stomach, knocking us flat and blinding us for the moment. A splinter struck Talbot on his tin hat, grazing his skin. Behind us one of the orderlies screamed and we rushed back to him. He had been hit below the knee and his leg was nearly severed. We tied him up and managed to get him back to the Australian aid-post. Two of the original four stretcher-bearers had been blown up a few minutes before. But the remaining two were carrying on with their work as though nothing had happened. Here he was band-aged and started on his way for the dressing-station.

[86] Far across the snow, we saw three more tanks plodding back toward the rear. Little by little, we gained ground until we reached a more sheltered area where we could make greater speed. We were feverishly anxious to know the fate of the crew of the burning tank. "Whose tank was it?" was on every tongue. We met other wounded men being helped back; those with leg wounds were being support-ed by others less seriously wounded. They could tell us nothing. They had been with the infantry and only knew that two tanks were right on the other side of the village.

A moment or two later, Talbot started running toward two men, one of whom was supporting the other. The wounded man proved to be the Sergeant of the tank we had seen on fire. We hurried up to him. He was hurt in the leg. So, instead of firing questions at him, we kept quiet and accompanied him back to the dressing-station.

Later we heard the tragic news that it was Gould's tank that had burned up. None of us talked much about it. It did not seem real. [87] They had got stuck in the German wire. A crump had hit them and fired the petrol tank. That was the end. Two men, the Sergeant and another, escaped from the tank. The others perished with it. We tried to comfort each other by repeated assurances that they must all have lost consciousness quickly from the fumes of the petrol before they suffered from fire. But it was small consolation. Every one had liked Gould and every one would miss him.

We waited at Brigade Headquarters for the others to return. A Tank Commander from another Company was brought in, badly wounded and looking ghastly, but joking with every one, as they carried him along on a stretcher. His tank had been knocked out and they had saved their guns and gone on with the infantry. He had been the last to leave the tank, and as he had stepped out to the ground, a shell exploded directly beneath him, taking off both of his legs below the knee.

The last of the tanks waddled wearily in and the work of checking-up began. All were accounted for but two. Their fate still remains [88] a secret. Our theory was that they had gone too far ahead and had entered the village in back of the German lines; that the infantry had not been able to keep up with them, and that they had been captured. Two or three days afterwards an airman told us that he had seen, on the day of the battle, two tanks far ahead of the infantry and that they appeared to be stranded. Weeks later we attacked at the point where the tanks had been, and on some German prisoners whom we took, we found several photographs of these identical tanks. Then one day, when we had stopped wondering about them, a Sergeant in our Company received a letter from one of the crew of the missing machines, saying that he was a prisoner in Germany. But of the officers we have never heard to this day.

We sat around wearily, waiting for the motor lorries which were to take some of us back to B— —. Years seemed to have been crowded into the hours that had elapsed. Talbot glanced at his watch. It was still only eight o'clock in the morning. Again he experienced the [89] feeling of incredulity that comes to one who has had much happen in the hours between dawn and early morning and who discovers that the day has but just begun. He had thought it must be three o'clock in the afternoon, at least.

The lorries arrived eventually, and took those who had no tanks, back to B— —. The others brought the "Willies" in by the evening.

[90]

VII

THE SECOND BATTLE ToC

Ten days had now elapsed since that day when we had gone back to B— — with the officers and men who had survived. We had enjoyed every minute of our rest and once more were feeling fit. The remainder of the Company had been divided up into crews. The "Willies" themselves had had the best of care and attention.

Most important of all, to the childish minds of that part of the British Army which we represented, we had given another concert which had been an even greater success than the first. The Old Bird and Borwick had excelled themselves. We were convinced that something was wrong with a Government that would send two such artists to the front! They should be at home, writing "words and music" that would live forever.

Toward the end of the week, plans for another attack were arranged. This time it was [91] to take place at C— —, about five miles north of N— —. We were told that this was to be a "big show" at last. Part of the Hindenburg Line had been taken, and part was still in the hands of the enemy. It had been decided, therefore, that this sector of the line, and the village behind it, must be captured. Our share in the business consisted of a few tanks to work with the infantry. Two of us went up three days before to arrange the plans with the Divisional Commander. We wandered up into the Hindenburg Line as close as we could get to the Boche, to see what the ground was like, and to decide if possible on the routes for the tanks. In the line were innumerable souvenirs. We found the furniture that the Germans had taken out of the villages on their retirement, and had used to make their line more comfortable.

We found, too, an extraordinary piece of engineering. A tunnel about ten miles long ran underneath the whole of the Hindenburg Line. It was about thirty or forty feet down, and had been dug, we heard, by Russian prisoners. The tunnel was about six feet wide and about five [92] feet high. It had been roughly balked in with timber, and at every twenty yards, a shaft led out of the tunnel up into the trench. Borwick found a large mirror which he felt could not be wasted under the circumstances. He could not resist its charm, so he started lugging it back the six miles to camp. It was very heavy and its charm had decreased greatly by the time he reached camp and found that no one could make any use of it.

The day of the attack was still undecided, and in order to be quite ready when it should come off, we left B— — with the tanks one evening and took them up to Saint-L— —, a little place about three thousand yards away from the Hindenburg Line. Here we staged them behind a railway embankment, underneath a bridge that had been partially blown up. This was the same embankment, as a matter of fact, behind which, four or five miles away, the Australian dressing-station had been established in the last battle.

Here we spent two or three days tuning up the machines, and many of our leisure moments [93] in watching a howitzer battery which was just beside us. This was fascinating. If you stand by the gun when it is fired, you can see the shell leave the muzzle, and watch the black mass shoot its seven or eight thousand yards until it becomes a small speck and finally vanishes just before it hits the ground.

We also made an interesting collection of German and English shell-cases. These cases are made of brass, and the four-fives, especially, in the opinion of some people, make very nice rose-bowls when they are polished, with wire arranged inside to hold the blossoms. Weird music could be heard issuing from our dugout at times, when we gave an impromptu concert, by putting several of these shell-cases on a log of wood and playing elaborate tunes on them with a bit of stone.

All this merry-making came to an end, though. One day we received word that the attack was to come off the next morning. Then began the preparations in earnest and the day went with a rush. At this part of the Hindenburg Line, it was very easy to lose one's way, especially at [94] night. The tanks were scheduled to start moving up at ten o'clock. Talbot and the Old Bird, with several men, set out at about eight, and arranged for marks to guide the machines.

We had just reached a part of the Hindenburg Line which was now in our possession, and were near an ammunition dump, when shells began to fall around us. They were not near enough to do us any harm, and we continued our work, when one dropped into the ammunition dump and exploded. In an instant the whole dump was alight. It was like some terrible and giant display of pyrotechnics. Gas shells, Verey lights, and stink bombs filled the air with their nauseous odors. Shells of all sizes blew up and fell in steely splinters. The noise was deafening. Cursing our luck, we waited until it died down into a red, smouldering mass, and then edged up cautiously to continue our work. By this time, Borwick's tank came up, and he emerged, with a broad smile on his face.

"Having a good time?" he asked genially.

[95] There was a frozen silence, excepting for his inane laughter. He made a few more irritating remarks which he seemed to think were very funny, and then he disappeared inside his tank and prepared to follow us. We had gone ahead a couple of hundred yards when we heard bombs exploding, and looking back we saw the tank standing still, with fireworks going off under one of her tracks. Presently the noise ceased, and after waiting a moment we strolled back. As we reached the tank, Borwick and the crew came tumbling out, making the air blue with their language. They had run over a box of bombs, the only thing that had survived the fire in the ammunition dump, and one of the tracks was damaged. To repair it meant several hours' hard work in the cold in unpleasant proximity to the still smouldering dump. Over Talbot's face spread a broad smile.

"Having a good time?" he asked pleasantly of Borwick.

Infuriated growls were his only answer. He moved on with his men, while Borwick and his crew settled down to work.

[96] The night was fortunately dark. They went slowly forward and brought the route almost up to within calling distance of the Germans. The Verey lights, shattering the darkness over No Man's Land, did not disclose them to the enemy. Suddenly, a Boche machine gun mechanically turned its attentions toward the place where they were working. With a tightening of every muscle, Talbot heard the slow whisper of the gun. As it turned to sweep the inter-

vening space between the lines, the whisper rose to a shirring hiss. The men dropped to the ground, flattening themselves into the earth. But Talbot stood still. Now, if ever, was the time when an example would count. If they all dropped to the ground every time a machine gun rattled, the job would never be done. So, hands in his pockets, but with awful "wind up," he waited while the soft patter of the bullets came near and the patter quickened into rain. As it reached him, the rain became a fierce torrent, stinging the top of the parapet behind them as the bullets tore by viciously a few inches above his head. Then as it passed, it [97] dropped into a patter once more and finally dropped away in a whisper. Talbot suddenly realized that his throat was aching, but that he was untouched by the storm. The men slowly got to their feet and continued their work in silence. Although the machine gun continued to spatter bullets near them all through the hours they were working, not once again did the men drop when they heard the whisper begin. The job was finally done and they filed wearily back.

The attack was timed to come off at dawn. An hour before, while it was still as black as pitch, the tanks moved again for their final starting-point. McKnutt's machine was the first to go.

"Cheero, McKnutt," we said as he clambered in. "Good luck!"

The men followed, some through the top and some through the side. The doors and portholes were closed, and in a moment the exhaust began to puff merrily. The tank crawled forward and soon disappeared into the blackness.

She had about fifteen hundred yards to go, [98] parallel with the Hindenburg Line, and several trenches to cross before coming up with the enemy. We had planned that the tanks would take about three quarters of an hour to reach their starting-point, and that soon after they arrived there, the show would begin.

Since it was still dark and the attack had not commenced, McKnutt and his first driver opened the windows in front of them. They looked out into impenetrable gloom. It was necessary to turn their headlights on, and with this help, they crawled along a little more securely. A signal from the driver, and they got into top gear. She bumped along, over shell-holes and mine-craters at the exhilarating speed of about four miles an hour, and then arrived at the first trench to be crossed. It was about ten feet wide with high banks on each side.

"One up!" signals the driver. The gears-men get into first gear, and the tank tilts back as it goes up one side of the trench. Suddenly she starts tipping over, and the driver takes out his clutch and puts on his brake hard. McKnutt yells out, "Hold tight!" and the [99] tank slides gently down with her nose in the bottom of the trench. The driver lets in his clutch again, the tank digs her nose into the other side and pulls herself up slowly, while her tail dips down into the bottom of the trench. Then comes the great strain as she pulls herself bodily out of the trench until she balances on the far side.

It was now no longer safe to run with lights. They were snapped off. Once more the darkness closed around them, blacker than ever. They could no longer find their route, and McKnutt jumped out, walking ahead with the tank lumbering along behind. Twice he lost his way and they were obliged to wait until he found it again. Then, to his intense relief, the moon shone out with a feeble light. It was just enough to illumine faintly the ground before them and McKnutt reëntered the tank, and started on.

Their route ran close to the sides of an old quarry and they edged along cautiously. McKnutt, with his eyes glued to the front, decided that they must have already passed the end of [100] the quarry. That would mean that they were not far from the spot where they were to wait for the signal to go into action. The moon had again disappeared behind the clouds, but he did not consider it worth while to get out again. The journey would be over in a few minutes.

Suddenly, his heart took a great dive and he seemed to stop breathing. He felt the tank balance ever so slightly. Staring with aching eyes through the portholes, he saw that they were on the edge of the old quarry, with a forty-foot drop down its steep sides before them. The black depth seemed bottomless. The tank was slipping over. When she shot down they would all be killed from concussion alone.

His heart was pounding so that he could hardly speak. But the driver, too, had seen the danger.

"For God's sake, take out your clutch and put your brake on!" McKnutt yelled, his voice almost drowned by the rattle and roar inside the tank. The man kept his head. As the tail of the tank started tipping up, he managed somehow with the brakes to hold her on the [101] edge. For a second or two, she swayed there. She seemed to be unable to decide whether to kill them or not. The slightest crumbling of the earth or the faintest outside movement against the tank would precipitate them over the edge. The brakes would not hold them for long. Then the driver acted. Slowly he put his gears in reverse, keeping the brake on hard until the engine had taken up the strain. Slowly she moved back until her tail bumped on the ground, and she settled down. Neither McKnutt nor his driver spoke. They pushed back their tin hats and wiped their foreheads.

McKnutt glanced back at the men in the rear of the tank. They, of course, had been unable to see out, and had no idea of what they had escaped. Now that the danger was passed, he felt an unreasonable annoyance that none of them would ever know what he and the driver had gone through in those few moments. Then the feeling passed, he signalled, "Neutral left," the gearsman locked his left track, and the tank swung over, passing safely by the perilous spot.

[102] They settled down now to a snail's pace, shutting off their engine, as the Germans could not be more than one hundred and fifty or two hundred yards away. Running at full speed, the engine would have been heard by them. In a few moments, they arrived at their appointed station. McKnutt glanced at his watch. They had only a few moments to wait. The engine was shut off and they stopped.

The heat inside the tank was oppressive. McKnutt and James opened the top, and crawled out, the men following. They looked around. The first streaks of light were beginning to show in the sky. A heavy silence hung over everything—the silence that always precedes a bombardment. Presumably, only the attacking forces feel this. Even the desultory firing seems to have faded away. All the little ordinary noises have ceased. It is a sickening quiet, so loud in itself that it makes one's heart beat quicker. It is because one is listening so intensely for the guns to break out that all other sounds have lost their significance. One seems to have become all [103] ears — to have no sense of sight or touch or taste or smell. All seem to have become merged in the sense of hearing. The very air itself seems tense with listening. Only the occasional rattle of a machine gun breaks the stillness. Even this passes unnoticed.

Slowly the minute-hand crept round to the half-hour, and the men slipped back into their steel home. Doors were bolted and portholes shut, save for the tiny slits in front of officer and driver, through which they peered. The engine was ready to start. The petrol was on and flooding. They waited quietly. Their heavy breathing was the only sound. The minute-hand reached the half-hour.

With the crash and swish of thousands of shells, the guns smashed the stillness. Instantly, the flash of their explosion lit up the opposite trenches. For a fraction of a second the thought came to McKnutt how wonderful it was that man could produce a sound to which Nature had no equal, either in violence or intensity. But the time was for action and not for reflection.

[104] "Start her up!" yelled out McKnutt.

But the engine would not fire.

"What the devil's the matter?" cried James.

A bit of tinkering with the carburetor, and the engine purred softly. Its noise was drowned in the pandemonium raging around them. James let in the clutch, and the monster moved forward on her errand of destruction.

Although it was not light enough to distinguish forms, the flashes of the shell-fire and the bursts from the shrapnel lit up that part of the Hindenburg Line that lay on the other side of the barrier. One hundred and fifty yards, and the tank was almost on top of the barricade. Bombs were exploding on both sides. McKnutt slammed down the shutters of the portholes in front of him and his driver. "Bullets," he said shortly.

"One came through, I think, sir," James replied. With the portholes shut, there was no chance for bullets to enter now through the little pin-points directly above the slits in the shutters. In order to see through these, it is necessary to place one's eye directly against

[105] the cold metal. They are safe, for if a bullet does hit them, it cannot come through, although it may stop up the hole.

Suddenly a dull explosion was heard on the roof of the tank.

"They're bombing us, sir!" cried one of the gunners. McKnutt signalled to him, and he opened fire from his sponson. They plunged along, amid a hail of bullets, while bombs exploded all around them.

McKnutt and James, with that instinctive sense of direction which comes to men who control these machines, felt that they were hovering on the edge of the German trench. Then a sudden flash from the explosion of a huge shell lit up the ground around them, and they saw four or five gray-clad figures, about ten yards away, standing on the parapet hysterically hurling bombs at the machine. They might as well have been throwing pebbles. Scornfully the tank slid over into the wide trench and landed with a crash in the bottom. For a moment she lay there without moving. The Germans thought she was stuck. They [106] came running along thinking to grapple with her. But they never reached her, for at once the guns from both sides opened fire and the Germans disappeared.

The huge machine dragged herself up the steep ten-foot side of the trench. As she neared the top, it seemed as if the engine would not take the final pull. James took out his clutch, put his brake on hard, and raced the engine. Then letting the clutch in with a jerk, the tank pulled herself right on to the point of balance, and tipped slowly over what had been the parapet of the German position.

Now she was in the wire which lay in front of the trench. McKnutt signalled back, "Swing round to the left," parallel to the lay of the line. A moment's pause, and she moved forward relentlessly, crushing everything in her path, and sending out a stream of bullets from every turret to any of the enemy who dared to show themselves above the top of the trench.

At the same time our own troops, who had waited behind the barricade to bomb their way [107] down, from traverse to traverse, rushed over the heap of sandbags, tangled wire, wood, and dead men which barred their way. The moral effect of the tank's success, and the terror which she inspired, cheered our infantry on to greater efforts. The tank crew were, at the time, unaware of the infantry's action, as none of our own men could be seen. The only indication of the fact was the bursting of the bombs which gradually moved from fire bay to fire bay.

The Corporal touched McKnutt on the arm.

"I don't believe our people are keeping up with us, sir," he said. "They seem to have been stopped about thirty yards back."

"All right," McKnutt answered. "We'll turn round."

McKnutt and James opened their portholes to obtain a clearer view. Five yards along to the left, a group of Germans were holding up the advancing British. They had evidently prepared a barricade in case of a possible bombing attack on our part, and this obstacle, together with a fusillade of bombs which met them, prevented our troops from pushing on. [108] McKnutt seized his gun and pushed it through the mounting, but found that he could not swing round far enough to get an aim on the enemy. But James was in a better position. He picked the gray figures off, one by one, until the bombing ceased and our own men jumped over the barricade and came down among the dead and wounded Germans.

Then a sudden and unexplainable sense of disaster caused McKnutt to look round. One of his gunners lay quite still on the floor of the tank, his back against the engine, and a stream of blood trickling down his face. The Corporal who stood next to him pointed to the sights in the turret and then to his forehead, and McKnutt realized that a bullet must have slipped in through the small space, entering the man's head as he looked along the barrel of his gun. There he lay, along one side of the tank between the engine and the sponson. The Corporal tried to get in position to carry on firing with his own gun, but the dead body impeded his movements.

There was only one thing to do. The Corporal looked questioningly at McKnutt and [109] pointed to the body. The officer nodded quickly, and the left gearsman and the Corporal dragged the body and propped it up against the door. Immediately the door flew open. The back of the corpse fell down and half the body lay hanging out, with its legs still caught on the floor. With feverish haste they lifted the legs and threw them out, but the weight of the body balanced them back again through the still open door. The men were desperate. With a tremendous heave they turned the dead man upside down, shoved the body out and slammed the door shut. They were just in time. A bomb exploded directly beneath the sponson, where the dead body had fallen. To every man in the tank came a feeling of swift gratitude that the bombs had caught the dead man and not themselves.

They ploughed across another trench without dropping into the bottom, for it was only six feet wide. Daylight had come by now and the enemy was beginning to find that his brave efforts were of no avail against these monsters of steel.

[110] All this time the German guns had not been silent. McKnutt's tank crunched across the ground amid a furious storm of flying earth and splinters. The strain was beginning to be felt. Although one is protected from machine-gun fire in a tank, the sense of confinement is, at times, terrible. One does not know what is happening outside his little steel prison. One often cannot see where the machine is going. The noise inside is deafening; the heat terrific. Bombs shatter on the roof and on all sides. Bullets spatter savagely against the walls. There is an awful lack of knowledge; a feeling of blind helplessness at being cooped up. One is entirely at the mercy of the big shells. If a shell hits a tank near the petrol tank, the men may perish by fire, as did Gould, without a chance of escape. Going down with your ship seems pleasant compared to burning up with your tank. In fighting in the open, one has, at least, air and space.

McKnutt, however, was lucky. They could now see the sunken road before them which was their objective. Five-nines were dropping [111] around them now. It was only a matter of moments, it seemed, when they would be struck.

"Do you think we shall make it?" McKnutt asked James.

"We may get there, but shall we get back? That's the question, sir."

McKnutt did not answer. They had both had over two years' experience of the accuracy of the German artillery. And they did not believe in miracles. But they had their orders. They must simply do their duty and trust to luck.

They reached the sunken road. The tank was swung around. Their orders were to reach their objective and remain there until the bombers arrived. McKnutt peered out. No British were in sight, and he snapped his porthole shut. Grimly they settled down to wait.

The moments passed. Each one seemed as if it would be their last. Would the infantry never come? Would there be any sense in just sitting there until a German shell annihilated them if the infantry never arrived? Had they been pushed back by a German rush? Should [112] he take it upon himself to turn back? McKnutt's brain whirled.

Then, after hours, it seemed, of waiting, around the corner of a traverse, he saw one of the British tin hats. Nothing in the world could have been a happier sight. A great wave of relief swept over him. Three or four more appeared. Realizing that they, too, had reached their objective, they stopped and began to throw up a rough form of barricade. More men poured in. The position was consolidated, and there was nothing more for the tank to do.

They swung round and started back. Two shells dropped about twenty yards in front of them. For a moment McKnutt wondered whether it would be well to change their direction. "No, we'll keep right on and chance it," he said aloud. The next moment a tremendous crash seemed to lift the tank off the ground. Black smoke and flying particles filled the tank. McKnutt and James looked around expecting to see the top of the machine blown off. But nothing had happened inside, and no one was injured. Although shells continued to [113] fall around them and a German machine gun raged at them, they got back safely.

A TANK BRINGING IN A CAPTURED GERMAN GUN UNDER PROTECTION OF CAMOUFLAGE ToList

Brigade Headquarters, where McKnutt reported, was full of expectancy. Messages were pouring in over the wires. The men at the telephones were dead beat, but cool and collected.

"Any news of the other 'busses?" McKnutt asked eagerly. The Buzzers shook their heads wearily. He rushed up to a couple of men who were being carried to a dressing-station.

"Do you fellows know how the tanks made out?" he asked.

One of them had seen two of the machines on the other side of the German line, he said. In answer to the questions which were fired at him he could only say that the tanks had pushed on beyond the German front line.

Then on the top of the hill, against the sky-line, they saw a little group of three or four men. James recognized them.

70

"Why, there's Sergeant Browning and Mr. Borwick, sir," he said. "What's happened to their tank, I wonder?" He and McKnutt hurried over to meet them.

[114] Borwick smiled coolly.

"Hullo!" he said in his casual manner.

"What's happened to your 'bus?" "What did you do?" was fired at him.

"We got stuck in the German wire, and the infantry got ahead of us," he said. "We pushed on, and fell into a nest of three machine guns. They couldn't hurt us, of course, and the Boches finally ran away. We knocked out about ten of them, and just as we were going on and were already moving, we suddenly started twisting around in circles. What do you think had happened? A trench mortar had got us full in one of our tracks, and the beastly thing broke. So we all tumbled out and left her there."

"Didn't you go on with the infantry?" asked McKnutt.

"No. They'd reached their objective by that time," Borwick replied, "so we saved the tank guns, and I pinched the clock. Then we strolled back, and here we are," he concluded.

Talbot joined the group as he finished.

"But where's the rest of your crew?" he asked.

Borwick said quietly: "Jameson and [115] Corporal Fiske got knocked out coming back." He lit a cigarette and puffed at it.

There was silence for a moment.

Then Talbot said, "Bad luck; have you got their pay-books?"

"No, I forgot them," Borwick answered.

But his Sergeant handed over the little brown books which were the only tangible remains of two men who had gone into action that morning. The pay-books contained two or three pages on which were jotted down their pay, with the officer's signature. They had been used as pocket-books, and held a few odd letters which the men had received a few days before. Talbot had often been given the pay-books of men in his company who were killed, but he never failed to be affected when he discovered the letters and little trifles which had meant so much to the men who had carried them, and which now would mean so much to those whom they had left behind.

In silence they went back to McKnutt's tank and sat down, waiting for news. Scraps of information were beginning to trickle in.

[116] "Have gained our objective in X Wood. Have not been counter-attacked."

"Cannot push on owing to heavy machine-gun fire from C$--$."

"Holding out with twenty men in trench running north from Derelict Wood. Can I have reinforcements?"

These were the messages pouring in from different points on the lines of attack. Sometimes the messages came in twos and threes. Sometimes there were minutes when only a wild buzzing could be heard and the men at the telephones tried to make the buzzing intelligible.

The situation cleared up finally, however. Our troops had, apparently, gained their objectives along the entire line to the right. On the left the next Brigade had been hung up by devastating machine-gun fire. As McKnutt and Talbot waited around for news and fresh orders, one of their men hurried down and saluted.

He brought the news that the other three tanks had returned, having reached their [117] objectives. Two had but little opposition and the infantry had found no difficulty in gaining their points of attack. The third tank, however, had had three men wounded at a "pill-box." These pill-boxes are little concrete forts which the German had planted along his line. The walls are of ferro concrete, two to three feet thick. As the tank reached the pill-box, two Germans slipped out of the rear door. Three of the tank crew clambered down and got inside the pill-box. In a moment the firing from inside ceased, and presently the door flew open. Two British tank men, dirty and grimy, escorting ten Germans, filed out. The Germans had their hands above their heads, and when ordered to the rear they went with the greatest alacrity. One of the three Englishmen was badly wounded; the other two were only slightly injured, but they wandered down to the dressing-station, with the hope that "Blighty" would soon welcome them.

Although Talbot had his orders to hold the tanks in readiness in case they were needed, no necessity arose, and after a few hours' waiting, [118] the Major sent word to him to start the tanks back to the embankment, there to be kept for the next occasion. Better still, the men were to be taken back to B— — in the motor lorries, just as they had been after the first battle. Water, comparative quiet, blankets, — these were the luxuries that lay before them.

As he sat crowded into the swaying motor lorry that lurched back along the shell-torn road to B— —, Talbot slipped his hand into his pocket. He touched a cheque-book, a package of cigarettes, and a razor. Then he smiled. They were the final preparations he had made that morning before he went into action. After all he had not needed them, but one never could tell, one might be taken prisoner. One needed no such material preparations against the possibility of death, but a prisoner — that was different.

The cheque-book had been for use in a possible gray prison camp in the land of his enemies. Cheques would some time or other reach his English bank and his people would know that he was, at least, alive. The cigarettes were [119] to keep up his courage in the face of whatever disaster might befall him.

And the razor? Most important of all.

The razor was to keep, bright and untarnished, the traditions and prestige of the British Army!

[120]

VIII

REST AND DISCIPLINE

We stayed in that region of the Front for a few more weeks, preparing for any other task that might be demanded of us. One day the Battalion received its orders to pack up, to load the tanks that were left over, and to be ready for its return to the district in which we had spent the winter.

We entrained on a Saturday evening at A— —, and arrived at St.-P— — at about ten o'clock on Sunday night. From there a twelve-mile march lay before us to our old billets in B— —. As may well be imagined, the men, though tired, were in high spirits. We simply ate up the distance, and the troops disguised their fatigue by singing songs. There were two which appeared to be favorites on this occasion.

One, to the tune of "The Church's One Foundation," ran as follows: —

> "We are Fred Karno's [1] Army,
> [121] The ragtime A.S.C., [2]
> We cannot work, we do not fight,
> So what ruddy use are we?
> And when we get to Berlin,
> The Kaiser he will say,
> Hoch, hoch, mein Gott!
> What a ruddy rotten lot,
> Is the ragtime A.S.C."

The other was a refrain to the tune of a Salvation Army hymn, "When the Roll is called up Yonder": —

> "When you wash us in the water,
> That you washed your dirty daughter,
> Oh! then we will be much whiter!

We'll be whiter than the whitewash on the wall."

Eventually the companies arrived in the village at all hours of the morning. No one was up. We saw that the men received their meals, which had been prepared by the cooks who had gone ahead in motor lorries. They did not spend much time over the food, for in less than half an hour "K" billets—the same Hospice de Ste. Berthe— were perfectly quiet. [122] We then wandered away with our servants, to be met at each of our houses by hastily clad landladies, with sleep in their eyes and smoking lamps or guttering candles in their hands.

The next morning the Company paraded at half-past nine, and the day was spent in reforming sections, in issuing new kits to the men, and in working the rosters for the various courses. On Tuesday, just as breakfast was starting, an orderly brought a couple of memorandums from Battalion Orderly Room for McKnutt and Borwick.

No one watched them read the chits, but Talbot, glancing up from his plate, saw a look on Borwick's face. It was a look of the purest joy.

"What is it?" he said.

"Leave, my God!" replied Borwick; "and McKnutt's got it too."

"When are you going? To-day?" shouted the Old Bird.

"Yes; there's a car to take us to the station in a quarter of an hour."

They both left their unfinished breakfasts [123] and tore off to their billets. There it was but a matter of moments to throw a few things into their packs. No one ever takes any luggage when going on leave. They tore back to the mess to leave instructions for their servants, and we strolled out *en masse* to see the lucky fellows off.

The box-body drew away from where we were standing. We watched it grow smaller and smaller down the long white road, and turned back with regrets and pleasure in our hearts. With regrets, that we ourselves were not the lucky ones, and knowing that for some of us leave would never come; with pleasure, because one is always glad that a few of the deserving reap a small share of their reward.

Then, strolling over to the Parade Ground, we heard the "Five Minutes" sounding. Some dashed off to get their Sam Brownes, others called for their servants to wipe a few flecks of dust from their boots and puttees.

When the "Fall In" began, the entire Company was standing "At Ease" on the Parade Ground. As the last note of the call sounded, [124] the whole parade sprang to "Attention," and the Major, who had been standing on the edge of the field, walked forward to inspect.

Every morning was spent in this manner, except for those who had special courses to follow. We devoted all our time and attention to "Forming Fours" in as perfect a manner as possible; to saluting with the greatest accuracy and fierceness; and to unwearying repetition of every movement and detail, until machinelike precision was attained.

All that we were doing then is the very foundation and essence of good discipline. Discipline is the state to which a man is trained, in order that under all circumstances he shall carry out without secondary reasoning any order that may be given him by a superior. There is nothing of a servile nature in this form of obedience. Each man realizes that it is for the good of the whole. By placing his implicit confidence in the commands of one of a higher rank than his own, he gives an earnest of his ability to himself command at some future time. It is but another proof of the old adage, [125] that the man who obeys least is the least fitted to command.

Copyright by Underwood & Underwood, N.Y.

A BRITISH TANK IN THE LIBERTY LOAN PARADE IN NEW YORK ToList

When this war started, certain large formations, with the sheer lust for fighting in their blood, did not, while being formed, realize the absolute necessity of unending drill and inspection. Their first cry was, "Give us a rifle, a bayonet, and a bomb, show us how to use them, and we will do the rest." Acting upon this idea, they flung themselves into battle, disregarding the iron rules of a preliminary training. At first their very impetus and courage carried them over incredible obstacles. But after a time, and as their best were killed off, the original blaze died down, and the steady flame of ingrained discipline was not there to take the place of burning enthusiasm. The terrible waste and useless sacrifice that ensued showed only too plainly that even the greatest individual bravery is not enough.

In this modern warfare there are many trials and experiences un-imagined before, which wear down the actual will-power of the men who undergo them. When troops are forced [126] to sit in a trench under the most terrific shell-fire, the nerve-racking noise, the

78

sight of their comrades and their defences being blown to atoms, and the constant fear that they themselves will be the next to go, all deprive the ordinary mind of vital initiative. Having lost the active mental powers that a human being possesses, they are reduced to the level of machines. The officers and non-commissioned officers, on whom the responsibility of leadership rests, have that spur to maintain their equilibrium, but the private soldiers, who have themselves only to think of, are the most open to this devastating influence. If these machines are to be controlled, as they must be, by an exterior intelligence, they must obey automatically, and if in the past automatic obedience has not been implanted, there is nothing to take its place.

The only means by which to obtain inherent response to a given order is so to train a man in minute details, by constant, inflexible insistence on perfection, that it becomes part of his being to obey without thinking.

[127] It must not be presumed that, in obtaining this almost inhuman reaction, all independent qualities are obliterated. For, though a man's mind is adjusted to carrying out, without questioning, any task that is demanded of him, yet in the execution of this duty he is allowed the full scope of his invention and initiative.

Thus, by this dull and unending routine, we laid the foundation of that inevitable success toward which we were slowly working.

When the Company dismissed, the Major, Talbot, and the Old Bird walked over to lunch together.

"Well, it's a great war, isn't it?" said the Major, turning to the other two.

"It's very nice to have got through a couple of shows, sir," replied Talbot. "What do you think about it, Old Bird?"

"Well, of course, war is all very well for those who like it. But give me the Base every time," answered the Old Bird, true to his reputation. Then, turning to the Major with his most ingratiating smile, he said, "By the way, sir, what about a few days in Boulogne?"

[128]

IX

A PHILOSOPHY OF WAR ToC

It has often been observed that if this war is to end war for all time, and if all the sacrifices and misery and suffering will help to prevent any recurrence of them, then it is well worth while.

In these days of immediate demands and quick results, this question is too vague and too far-reaching to bring instant consolation. Apart from that, too, it cannot decide whether any war, however great, can ever abolish the natural and primitive fighting instinct in man.

The source from which we must draw the justification for our optimism lies much nearer to hand. We must regard the effect that warring life has already produced upon each individual member of the nations who are and who are not engaged in it.

At the very heart of it is the effect on the man who is actually fighting. Take the case [129] of him who before the war was either working in a factory, who was a clerk in a business house, or who was nothing at all beyond the veriest loafer and bar-lounger. To begin with, he was perhaps purely selfish. The foundation of his normal life was self-protection. Whether worthless or worthy, whether hating or respecting his superiors, the private gain and comfort for himself and his was the object of his existence. He becomes a soldier, and that act alone is a conversion. His wife and children are cared for, it is true; but he himself, for a shilling a day, sells to his country his life, his health, his pleasures, and his hopes for the future. To make good measure he throws in cheerfulness, devotion, philosophy, humour, and an unfailing kindness. One man, for instance, sells up three grocery businesses in the heart of Lancashire, an ambition which it has taken him ten years to accomplish. Without a trace of bitterness he divorces himself from the routine of a lifetime, and goes out to France to begin life again at the very bottom of a new ladder. He who for years had many men under [130] him is now under all, and receives, unquestioningly, orders which in a different sphere he had been accustomed to give. Apart from the mere letter of obedience and discipline he gains a spirit of devotion and self-sacrifice, which turns the bare military instrument into a divine virtue. He may, for instance, take up the duties of an officer's servant. Immediately he throws himself whole-heartedly into a new form of selfless generosity, which leads him to a thousand ways of care and forethought, that even the tenderest woman could hardly conceive. The man who receives this unwavering devotion can only accept it with the knowledge that no one can deserve it, and that it is greater gain to him who gives than to him who takes.

What life of peace is there that produces this god-like fibre in the plainest of men? Why, indeed, is it produced in the life of war? It is because in war sordidness and petty worries are eliminated; because the one great and ever-present fear, the fear of death, reduces all other considerations to their proper values. The actual fear of death is always present, but this [131] fear itself cannot be sordid when men can meet it of their own free will and with the most total absence of cringing or of cowardice.

In commercial rivalry a man will sacrifice the friend of years to gain a given sum, which will insure him increased material comforts. In war a man will deliberately sacrifice the life for which he wanted those comforts, to save perhaps a couple of men who have no claim on him whatsoever. He who before feared any household calamity now throws himself upon a live bomb, which, even though he might escape himself, will without his action kill other men who are near it. This deed loses none of its value because of the general belief among soldiers that life is cheap. Other men's lives are cheap. One's own life is always very dear.

One of the most precious results has been the resurrection of the quality of admiration. The man who before the war said, "Why is he my master?" is now only too glad to accept a leader who is a leader indeed. He has learned that as his leader cannot do without him, so he cannot do without his leader, and although [132] each is of equal importance in the scheme of affairs, their positions in the scheme are different. He has learned that there is a higher equality than the equality of class: it is the equality of spirit.

This same feeling is reflected, more especially among the leaders of the men, in the complete disappearance of snobbishness. No such artificial imposition can survive in a life where inherent value automatically finds its level; where a disguise which in peace-time passed as superiority, now disintegrates when in contact with this life of essentials. For war is, above all, a reduction to essentials. It is the touchstone which proves the qualities of our youth's training. All those pleasures that formed the gamut of a young man's life either fall away completely or find their proper place. Sport, games, the open-air life, have taught him that high cheerfulness, through failure or success, which makes endurance possible. But the complicated, artificial pleasures of ordinary times have receded into a dim, unspoken background. The wholesomeness of the existence that he [133] now leads has taught him to delight in the most simple and natural of things. This throwing aside of the perversions and fripperies of an over-civilization has forced him to regard them with a disgust that can never allow him to be tempted again by their inducements of delight and dissipation. The natural, healthy desires which a man is sometimes inclined to indulge in are no longer veiled under a mask of hypocrisy. They are treated in a perfectly outspoken fashion as the necessary accompaniments to a hard, open-air life, where a man's vitality is at its best. In consequence of this, and as the result of the deepening of man's character which war inevitably produces, the sense of adventure and mystery which accompanied the fulfilment of these desires has disappeared, and with it to a great extent the desires themselves have assumed a far less importance.

In peace, and especially in war, the young man's creed is casualness. Not the casualness of carelessness, but that which comes from the knowledge that up to each given point he has [134] done his best. It is this fundamental peace of mind which comes to a soldier that forms the beauty of his life. The order received must be obeyed in its exact degree, neither more nor less; and the responsibility, though great, is clearly defined. Each man must use his individual intelligence within the scope of the part assigned to him. The responsibility differs in kind, but not in degree, and the last link of the chain is as important as the first. There can be no shirking or shifting, and, knowing this, each task is finished, rounded out, and put away. One might think that this made thought mechanical: but it is mechanical only in so far as each man's intelligence is concentrated on his own particular duty, and each part working in perfect order contributes to the unison through which the whole machine develops its power. Thus the military life induces in men a clearer and more accurate habit of thought, and teaches each one to do his work well and above all to do his own work only.

From this very simplicity of life, which brings out a calmness of mind and that equable [135] temperament that minor worries can no longer shake, springs the mental leisure which gives time for other and unaccustomed ideas. Men who wittingly, time and again, have faced but escaped death, will inevitably begin to think what death may mean. As the first lessons of obedience teach each man that he needs a leader to pass through a certain crisis, so the crisis of death, where man must pass alone, demands a still higher Leader. With the admission that no man is self-sufficient, that sin of pride, which is the strongest barrier between a man and his God, falls away. He is forced, if only in self-defence, to recognize that faith in some all-sufficient Power is the only thing that will carry him through. If he could cut away the thousand sins of thought, man would automatically find himself at faith. It is the central but often hidden point of our intelligence; and although there are a hundred roads that lead to it, they may be completely blocked. The clean flame of the disciplined life burns away the rubbish that chokes these roads, and faith becomes a nearer and more constant thing.

[136] The sadness of war lies in the loss of actual personalities, but it is only by means of these losses that this surrender can be attained.

It must not be thought that faith comes overnight as a free gift. It is a long and slow process of many difficult steps. There may be first the actual literal crumbling, unknown in peace-time, of one's solid surroundings, to be repeated perhaps again and again until the old habit of reliance upon them is uprooted. Then comes the realization that this life at the front has but two possible endings. The first is to be so disabled that a man's fighting days are over. The other is death. Instant death rather than a slow death from wounds. Every man hopes for a wound which will send him home to England. That, however, is only a respite, as his return to France follows upon his convalescence. The other most important step is the loss of one's friends. It is not the fact of actually seeing them killed, for in the chaos and tumult of a battle the mind hardly registers such impressions. One's only feeling is the purely primitive one of relief, that it is another and not one's self. It [137] is only afterwards, when the excitement is over, and a man realizes that again there is a space of life, for him, but not for his friend, that the loneliness and the loss are felt. He then says to himself, "Why am I spared when many better men have gone?" At first resentment swallows up all other emotions. In time, when this bitterness begins to pass, the belief that somehow this loss is of some avail, carries him a little farther on the road to faith. This all comes to the man who before the war believed that the world was made for his pleasure, and who treated life from that standpoint. All that he wanted he took without asking. Now, all that he has he gives without being asked.

Woman, too, gives more than herself. She gives her men, her peace of mind and all that makes her life worth living. The man after all may have little hope, but while he is alive he has the daily pleasures of health, vitality, excitement, and a thousand interests. A woman has but a choice of sorrows: the sorrow of unbearable suspense or the acceptance of the end.

Yet it needed this war to show again to [138] women what they could best do in life: to love their men, bear their children, care for the sick and suffering, and learn to endure. It has taught them also to accept from man what he is able or willing to give, and to admit a higher claim than their own. They have been forced to put aside the demands and exactions which they felt before were their right, and to accept loneliness and loss without murmur or question.

A woman who loses her son loses the supreme reason of her existence; and yet the day after the news has come, she goes back to her work for the sons of other women. If she has more sons to give she gives them, and faces again the eternal suspense that she has lived through before. The younger women, who in times of peace would have looked forward to an advantageous and comfortable marriage, will now marry men whom they may never see again after the ten days' honeymoon is over, and will unselfishly face the very real possibility of widowhood and lonely motherhood. They have had to learn the old lesson that work for others is the only cure for sorrow, and [139] they have learned too that it is the only cure for all those petty worries and boredoms which assailed them in times of peace. If they have learned this, then again one may say that war is worth while.

What effect has the war had upon those countries who in the beginning were not engaged in it? The United States, for instance, has for three years been an onlooker. The people of that country have had every opportunity to view, in their proper perspectives, the feelings and changes brought about among the men and women of the combatant countries. At first, the enormous casualties, the sufferings and the sorrow, led them to believe that nothing was worth the price they would have to pay, were they to enter into the lists. For in the beginning, before that wonderful philosophy of spirit and cheerfulness of outlook arose, and before the far-reaching effects of the sacrifice of loved ones could be perceived, there seemed to be little reason or right for such a train of desolation. They were perfectly justified, too, in thinking this, when insufficient time had elapsed [140] to enable them to judge of the immense, sweeping, beneficial effects that this struggle has produced in the moral fibre and stamina of the nations engaged.

It must be remembered that the horrors of the imagination are far worse than the realities. The men who fight and the women who tend their wounds suffer mentally far less than those who paint the pictures in their minds, from data which so very often are grossly exaggerated. One must realize that the hardships of war are merely transient. Men suffer untold discomforts, and yet, when these sufferings are over and mind and body are at ease for a while, they are completely forgotten. The only mark they leave is the disinclination to undergo them again. But on those who do not realize them in their actuality, they cause a far more terrifying effect.

Now, others, as well, have discovered that war's advantages outweigh so much its losses. They who with their own eyes had seen the wonderful fortitude with which men stand pain, and the amazing submission with which [141] women bear sorrow, returned full of zeal and enthusiasm, to carry the torch of this uplifting flame to their own countrymen.

Others will realize, too, that although one may lose one's best, yet one's worst is made better. The women will find that the characters of their men will become softened. The clear-cut essentials of a life of war must make the mind of man direct. It may be brutal in its simplicity, but it is clear and frank. Yet to counteract this, the continual sight of suffering bravely borne, the deep love and humility that the devotion of others unconsciously produces, bring about this charity of feeling, this desire to forgive and this moderation in criticism, which is so marked in those who have passed through the strenuous, searing realities of war. Since the thirty pieces of silver, no minted coin in the world has bought so much as has the King's shilling of to-day.

THE END